RESTORE

A GUIDED LENT JOURNAL FOR PRAYER AND MEDITATION

SR. MIRIAM JAMES HEIDLAND, SOLT

ILLUSTRATED BY VALERIE DELGADO

AVE MARIA PRESS AVE Notre Dame, Indiana

Nihil Obstat: Reverend Monsignor Michael Heintz, PhD
Censor Librorum
Imprimatur: Most Reverend Kevin C. Rhoades
Bishop of Fort Wayne–South Bend
Given at: Fort Wayne, Indiana, on 9 November 2021

The *Nihil Obstat* and *Imprimatur* are official declarations that a book or pamphlet is free of doctrinal or moral error. No implication is contained therein that those who have granted the *Nihil Obstat* or *Imprimatur* agree with its contents, opinions, or statements expressed.

Scripture quotations are from the *Revised Standard Version of the Bible—Second Catholic Edition (Ignatius Edition)*, copyright © 2006 National Council of the Churches of Christ in the United States of America. Used by permission. All rights reserved.

Texts contained in this work derived whole or in part from liturgical texts copyrighted by the International Commission on English in the Liturgy (ICEL) have been published here with the confirmation of the Committee on Divine Worship, United States Conference of Catholic Bishops. No other texts in this work have been formally reviewed or approved by the United States Conference of Catholic Bishops.

Excerpts from the English translation of *The Roman Missal* © 2010, International Commission on English in the Liturgy Corporation. All rights reserved.

Forgiveness Meditation on page 167 adapted from *Healing the Whole Person Workbook*, Bob Schuchts (Tallahassee, FL: John Paul II Healing Center).

Founded in 1865, Ave Maria Press is a ministry of the United States Province of Holy Cross.

www.avemariapress.com

Paperback: ISBN-13 978-1-64680-148-0

E-book: ISBN-13 978-1-64680-149-7

Cover and interior images © 2022 Valerie Delgado, paxbeloved.com.

Cover and text design by Brianna Dombo.

Printed and bound in the United States of America.

CONTENTS

THIRD WEEK OF LENT: THE ROOTS OF SIN

PART 3: ALMSGIVING
HEALING OUR RELATIONSHIP WITH OTHERS

FOURTH WEEK OF LENT: THE HEALING BALM OF ALMSGIVING

FIFTH WEEK OF LENT: THE JOURNEY OF FORGIVENESS

PART 4: SACRIFICE

*JESUS TAKES ON OUR SIN AND DEATH
AND RESTORES US TO LIFE*

HOLY WEEK, THE WEEK OF ALL WEEKS

INTRODUCTION

BY HIS HOLY
AND GLORIOUS WOUNDS,
MAY CHRIST THE LORD
GUARD US
AND PROTECT US. AMEN.

BLESSING OF THE FIRE AND
PREPARATION OF THE CANDLE
FROM THE EASTER VIGIL

The season of Lent stirs many things in our hearts. Some people love it, some people dislike it, and all of us know that we are supposed to somehow be transformed through it all. We often give up chocolate, alcohol, or meat. We try to practice mortification and remember that we are only pilgrims on this earth and that all things pass away. And while all these things are inherently good and important, I often wonder what is being engaged at the deeper level of our hearts.

Over and over again this season, we will be reminded of God's mercy, love, compassion, and protection. We will see love poured out and a heart pierced for our offenses. And over and over again, God will invite us to turn away from our sins and idols, and from fragmentation, darkness, death, and all the things that break us and lead us away from salvation.

Jesus is inviting us into his life—how he lives, thinks, and loves. He is showing us what it means to be truly alive and truly human. He is inviting us into his heart so that he can reveal ours and bring us into communion.

The journey you are about to make is dangerous, for if you truly follow the Lord into the desert, you will never be the same. If you enter into this time with him from the heart, you will emerge with a heart that has been changed. Yours will be a heart that sees more deeply, is pierced more easily, loves more strongly, and lives more passionately. Jesus will be etched into the crevices of your being.

I invite you to not self-censor during these days as you read the reflections and answer the reflection questions. Be very honest. Jesus has much to tell you; you need only say yes.

We can try to go around, underneath, or over the Cross, but the life that we so desperately desire is on the other side, time and time again, little by little. The only way is through.

So let us rise and be on our way.

SR. MIRIAM JAMES HEIDLAND

HOW TO USE
THIS JOURNAL

The *Restore* Lenten journal's combination of daily meditations, questions for reflection, journaling space, prayers, and beautiful original art is specially designed to draw you into a deeper, richer experience of Lent. It prepares you not only to walk with Jesus to Calvary but also to go with him into the desert, to receive his healing mercy, to practice forgiveness, and to meet Jesus in the Sacraments of Reconciliation and Holy Communion.

WHO IS *RESTORE* FOR?

Restore is for anyone who desires to experience the forty days of Lent as a healing journey that leads you to explore the crevices of your heart. The season of Lent is the ideal time to step back from your life and evaluate where you stand with God, yourself, and others. This Lenten journal provides a daily path to prayer, fasting, and almsgiving as avenues for healing and restoration.

Restore is perfect for use in groups; in fact, it was designed with that in mind. There's something special about taking this Lenten journey with a community—whether that community is your entire parish, a small group, or your family. Visit **www.avemariapress.com/restore** for more information about bulk discounts, a leader's guide, help with organizing a small group, videos from Sr. Miriam James Heidland discussing the theme for each week of Lent, and other resources to help you make the most of your time together with *Restore*.

You can also use *Restore* on your own, with the meditations and journaling prompts helping you draw nearer to God, hear his voice in new ways, and pour out your heart to him as you turn your attention daily to Jesus's journey to the Cross. You may find that this Lent, you're in special need of regular quiet times of connection with God; *Restore* is an excellent way to help you find that space each day.

HOW IS RESTORE ORGANIZED?

Restore is organized into four parts:

✤ In part 1, you'll focus on the idea of *prayer* as our primary way of connecting with God and healing your relationship with him. Everything in the spiritual life begins with prayer, so too does this journal.

✤ Part 2 leads you to reflect on *fasting* as an avenue for healing your relationships with yourself and your sin. The meditations in this part help you explore the roots of your sin and desires so that you can come to terms with your need for Jesus's healing mercy.

✤ In part 3, you'll focus on *almsgiving* as a practice that heals your relationships with others. The meditations in this part challenge you to reflect on how you can be a better companion to members in your family and community.

✤ Part 4—Holy Week—is a deep exploration of where your heart stands with God and how you can walk with him to Calvary, uniting your *sacrifices* with his. And then we rise with him on Easter Sunday, experiencing the fullness of all things.

Within each week, you'll encounter a simple daily pattern made up of the following parts:

✤ Each day opens with a *quotation* from a saint, a great teacher, scripture, or liturgical text in order to focus your thoughts on the key idea from the day's meditation.

✦ The *meditation* from Sr. Miriam James Heidland draws out a message from the liturgy, scripture, or the process of spiritual healing to help you experience the mercy and love of God this Lent.

✦ The *reflection* challenges you to ponder and journal in response to the meditation, helping you identify practical ways to live out the Lenten season more fully.

✦ Finally, after you've read and journaled, the closing *prayer* provides a starting point for your own requests and prayers of thanksgiving and praise to God.

HOW SHOULD I READ RESTORE?

This Lenten journal's daily format is flexible enough to accommodate any reader's preferences: If you're a morning person, you may want to start your day with *Restore*, completing the entire day's reading, reflection, journaling, and prayer first thing in the morning. Or you may find that you prefer to end your day by using *Restore* to focus your attention on Christ as you begin to rest from the day's activities. You may even decide to read and pray as a family in the morning and journal individually in the evening.

The key is to find what works for you, ensuring that you have time to read carefully, ponder deeply, write honestly, and connect intimately with the Lord in prayer.

Whatever approach you choose (and whether you decide to experience *Restore* with a group or on your own), be sure to visit **www.avemariapress.com/restore** for extra resources to help you get the most out of this special Lenten journey.

PART I
PRAYER

HEALING OUR RELATIONSHIP WITH GOD

FOR ME, PRAYER IS A SURGE OF
THE HEART; IT IS A SIMPLE LOOK
TURNED TOWARD HEAVEN, IT IS
A CRY OF RECOGNITION AND OF
LOVE, EMBRACING BOTH TRIAL
AND JOY.

ST. THÉRÈSE OF LISIEUX

WEEK OF ASH
WEDNESDAY

WEEK OF ASH WEDNESDAY

ASH WEDNESDAY

BUT YOU ARE MERCIFUL TO ALL,
FOR YOU CAN DO ALL THINGS,
AND YOU OVERLOOK MEN'S
SINS, THAT THEY MAY REPENT.
. . . YOU SPARE ALL THINGS, FOR
THEY ARE YOURS, O LORD WHO
LOVE THE LIVING.

WISDOM 11:23, 26

THE INNER ROOM

Here we begin, dear friends. Ash Wednesday. Our foreheads are marked with the blackness of death while the words "Repent and believe in the gospel" or "Remember that you are dust, and to dust you shall return" are spoken over us. Every single person, no matter their age or state in life, receives the same greeting, for we all are called to repent, believe, and remember. All things pass away and only the eternal remains.

We receive glimpses of this reality throughout our lives, but today we ponder it specifically as the door through which we follow Jesus out into the desert. The *Catechism* states that "interior repentance is a radical reorientation of our whole life, a return, a conversion to God with all our heart, an end of sin, a turning away from evil, with repugnance toward the evil actions we have committed" (*CCC* 1431). We must turn away from what wounds us, destroys us, and makes us sick and turn toward God who heals us, saves us, and makes us whole.

While other people may know certain things about us, and we may know ourselves to varying degrees, only the Lord knows us fully. He alone sees us in our fullness and wholeness and loves us completely. This is why we must go into the "inner room" with him, into the hidden place, so all can be revealed.

He is inviting us into an encounter with him, in the depths of our hearts, for that is where true transformation takes place.

REFLECT

Where are you in your heart and life right now? What is Jesus wanting to heal in you as you pray, fast, and give alms this Lent?

PRAY

*JESUS, HELP ME AS I BEGIN THIS
JOURNEY WITH YOU. GIVE ME AN
OPEN HEART, A WILLING SPIRIT, AND
THE COURAGE TO KEEP GOING, NO
MATTER WHAT. AMEN.*

WEEK OF ASH WEDNESDAY

THURSDAY

PROMPT OUR ACTIONS WITH
YOUR INSPIRATION, WE PRAY,
O LORD,
AND FURTHER THEM WITH
YOUR CONSTANT HELP,
THAT ALL WE DO MAY ALWAYS
BEGIN FROM YOU
AND BY YOU BE BROUGHT TO
COMPLETION.

COLLECT FOR MASS OF THE DAY

THE SCHOOL OF LOVE

Perhaps by now you have noticed some areas of your life that need attention this Lent. When you look at the traditional Lenten disciplines of prayer, fasting, and almsgiving, you may have chosen a few practices for each discipline that will help bring you into deeper freedom during this season. And that is what the disciplines are supposed to do—bring us into communion with God, ourselves, and others. As sin scatters and fragments, love brings us into communion and wholeness.

The roots of the words *discipline* and *disciple* are similar in meaning—student, training, learning. We are learning how love and the school of love never end.

During Lent, the Lord is calling us to something very intimate—far beyond the mere surface of "praying more" or "giving up dessert." He is calling us into union with him in the heart. This is why we must allow the Lord to prompt our actions with his inspiration and further them with his help. We are not making the journey of Lent on our own or from our own will. We are being led by the Lord as the Holy Spirit led Jesus out into the desert.

REFLECT

As you feel the Lord's gentle tug on your heart, where would the Lord like to encounter you this Lent? Is it to a place you've already decided or someplace new? Ask the Holy Spirit to show you.

_____

_____

_____

_____

_____

_____

_____

_____

_____

_____

_____

_____

_____

_____

_____

_____

_____

_____

_____

_____

_____

_____

_____

_____

_____

_____

_____

PRAY

*LORD, HELP ME TO HEAR AND TO BE
FAITHFUL TO YOUR INSPIRATIONS
THIS LENT. AMEN.*

WEEK OF ASH WEDNESDAY

FRIDAY

HEAR, O LORD, AND BE GRACIOUS
TO ME! O LORD, BE MY HELPER.

PSALM 30:10

YOUR HEART WITH JESUS

Thousands of books have been written on prayer, but I would like to offer the guiding quote from St. Thérèse (on the part I title page) for your heart during this time. For that is what it is. This is a journey about your heart with Jesus and your relationship with him. Each person's relationship with Christ is unique and unrepeatable. As God loves each of us in a way he loves no other person, so too we love God in a way that no one else loves God. The shape of our heart is precious to him; he knows the distinct contours that belong to us alone.

No one can ever exhaust prayer for it is a direct encounter with the eternal, endless, indescribably beautiful God. It is the simple act of two hearts coming together—listening, sharing, receiving, responding, being, loving. Prayer heals our relationship with God. Where we are shattered by sin and disorder, prayer draws us into the heart of God.

Prayer happens in good times and in bad, in sickness and in health, in activity and in silence, without ceasing.

This relationship of covenant and communion is initiated by God. Our response is just that—a response to the One who invites us and draws us. God is interested in what matters the most. As the *Catechism of the Catholic Church* reveals, "Whether prayer is expressed in words or gestures, it is the whole man who prays. . . . It is the *heart* that prays. If our heart is far from God, the words of the prayer are in vain" (*CCC* 2562).

There are so many beautiful and rich ways to pray, and we need them all, but it is our heart that needs to pray the most.

REFLECT

Ask God to bring to your heart a time when you experienced an encounter with him that was powerful and moving. It could be an experience in prayer, a direct answer to prayer, or an encounter with God in creation. What are you experiencing in your heart and mind as you recall his goodness and love for you there?

_____

_____

_____

_____

_____

_____

_____

_____

_____

_____

_____

_____

_____

_____

_____

_____

_____

_____

_____

_____

_____

_____

_____

_____

_____

_____

_____

_____

_____

PRAY

COME, HOLY SPIRIT. TEACH ME
HOW TO PRAY. AMEN.

WEEK OF ASH WEDNESDAY
SATURDAY

ANSWER ME, O LORD, FOR
YOUR MERCIFUL LOVE IS
GOOD; ACCORDING TO YOUR
ABUNDANT COMPASSION, TURN
TO ME.

PSALM 69:16

THE LORD'S
TENDER MERCY

As the Lord leads us into these first few days of Lent, you may already be noticing a few things in your life. You may have had a deeper revelation of an aspect of God's love for you. You may already be tired of your Lenten practices, or you may have concluded that a lot of things need to change (and quickly!) and you cannot possibly do this on your own. These are the very places we must go with Jesus. But how are we to do so?

We often hear the word *mercy*, but the true meaning of the word easily passes us by. Our English use of the word *mercy* is derived from the Latin word *misericordia*, with *miseriae* denoting "misery" and *cor* denoting "heart." Or more succinctly, the heart of God enters into our misery. God enters into the true misery of our sin, sorrow, and suffering, and he saves us, restores us, and redeems us.

He does not do this theoretically or from a distance. He does this incarnationally and personally through the person of Jesus Christ. He became one of us. God coming to us as a man changes everything—absolutely everything. Jesus comes in littleness, simplicity, poverty, and nakedness. He comes in strength, truth, power, and wisdom. The heart of God became man, a man like us in all things but sin. And still he takes on our sin to save us.

He lived. He suffered. He died. He rose. He holds nothing back. And he shares his life with us.

I am often overwhelmed by the beauty of Jesus Christ. His heart is for our misery and the restoration therein.

REFLECT

What is one situation in your life where you ache to receive the Lord's tender mercy?

_____

_____

_____

_____

_____

_____

_____

_____

_____

_____

_____

_____

_____

_____

_____

_____

_____

_____

_____

_____

_____

_____

_____

_____

_____

_____

PRAY

_FATHER, THANK YOU FOR GIVING
ME YOUR SON IN YOUR RICH MERCY.
RESTORE ME WHERE I NEED IT THE
MOST. AMEN._

FIRST WEEK
OF LENT
THE DESERT

FIRST WEEK OF LENT

SUNDAY

NO ONE WHO BELIEVES IN HIM
WILL BE PUT TO SHAME.

ROMANS 10:11

LAY ALL
THINGS BARE

On this first Sunday of Lent, we are led by the Spirit into the desert with Jesus. The desert is a forbidding place. Replete with scarcity, dryness, and dangerous wildlife. We often find ourselves recoiling from the invitation to follow Jesus into these places.

The beautiful thing about the desert, though, is that it lays all things bare and Christ goes before us. We do not go into the desert alone, and the Lord will not reveal anything to us that he does not also wish to attend to and heal.

In the desert, things become very clear. We see our idols—the things we grasp at for salvation other than God. We see where we hide behind our fig leaves of self-righteousness and shame. We see where our sin has wreaked havoc in our lives and in the lives of others.

We also see Jesus's immense love for us right there in those very places. Jesus Christ is led into the desert by the Holy Spirit to suffer every temptation we will ever face and to emerge victorious. Jesus Christ is Spirit who does not fail.

Sorely afflicted, he remains faithful. Sorely afflicted, he knows our hearts. Sorely afflicted, he draws close to us with his love to save us.

The desert is within our hearts. It is the most important and difficult journey that we will ever continually make.

REFLECT

What part of you enters willingly into the desert with Jesus? What part of you resists?

_____

_____

_____

_____

_____

_____

_____

_____

_____

_____

_____

_____

_____

_____

_____

_____

_____

_____

_____

_____

_____

_____

_____

_____

PRAY

*JESUS, GIVE ME CLARITY TO SEE MY
IDOLS AND SURRENDER THEM TO
YOU. AMEN.*

FIRST WEEK OF LENT

MONDAY

BEHOLD, NOW IS THE ACCEPT-
ABLE TIME; BEHOLD, NOW IS
THE DAY OF SALVATION.

2 CORINTHIANS 6:2

TAKE HIM AS
YOUR GUIDE

We have all had the experience of knowing that we need to do something about a situation and yet putting it off until another day. It's incredible to witness the lengths to which we will go in order to procrastinate or deflect, somehow hoping the situation will diffuse itself or that we won't have to face it!

Certainly there is a time for all things, and fear and compulsion are not ideal motives for change, but I believe we all have places deep within our hearts where the Lord is saying to us, "It's time now. Let's look at these things together. I am with you. You are never alone. It is time to allow these places to surface so you can be well."

Perhaps even reading those words triggers anxiety in your heart or tension in your stomach. Jesus is with you. He leads you into these places, little by little. This is why prayer and encounter from the heart is so important.

When people love each other, they can talk about anything. It may not be easy, and it may take time, but the truth can come out and be seen and experienced by the witness of love. It is the bond of authentic and everlasting love (covenant) that allows for the freedom for everything to come out upon the altar of our hearts with God. Jesus will not reject us.

Today, as you read this, is a very acceptable time.

REFLECT

What is one thing the Lord is inviting you to place upon the altar of your heart today?

_____

_____

_____

_____

_____

_____

_____

_____

_____

_____

_____

_____

_____

_____

_____

_____

_____

_____

_____

_____

_____

_____

_____

_____

PRAY

LORD, GIVE ME THE COURAGE TO BE HONEST ABOUT MY HEART, KNOWING YOU KNOW EVERYTHING AND YOU ARE WITH ME TO LEAD ME AND GUIDE ME. AMEN.

FIRST WEEK OF LENT

TUESDAY

LORD, YOU HAVE BEEN OUR
DWELLING PLACE IN ALL
GENERATIONS.

PSALM 90:1

TRUST IN HIS
FAITHFULNESS

Trust is an interesting reality. It's hard to earn, easy to lose, and something that we hold very dear. It is one thing to say that we trust someone, and it is an entirely different thing to actually trust them and to allow our heart to rest more deeply in that other person.

To trust someone is to rely on the integrity, ability, or strength of a person. It is to have confidence (*con* means "with," *fide* means "faith") in a person that they are who they say they are. It is to rely upon a person with the hope that they will be faithful to their promises and their word.

When we rely upon someone, it is like we put our "weight" upon them and release the need to control, grasp, manipulate, or self-protect. We are opening our heart and life in vulnerability (able to be wounded) and allowing another close to us, entrusting to them what matters the most to us. And this is why it is so scary to us. This is why when someone breaks our trust, often our first instinct is to make an inner vow of "I will never trust anyone again. I will never allow myself to be hurt again by being vulnerable." (We will reflect more on this in the coming weeks.)

Because the Lord knows how difficult it is for our broken humanity to trust and be trusted, he continually reveals to us over and over again who he truly is. From the beginning to the end of scripture is an unbroken revelation of who God is and, because of him, who we are.

God is faithful. Over and over again, he is faithful.

REFLECT

What is a concrete experience you have had of God's fidelity to you?

_____

_____

_____

_____

_____

_____

_____

_____

_____

_____

_____

_____

_____

_____

_____

_____

_____

_____

_____

_____

_____

_____

_____

_____

_____

PRAY

*JESUS, HELP ME TO TRUST YOU.
ILLUMINE THE PLACES IN MY HEART
WHERE I FEAR TO TRUST YOU AND BE
WITH ME THERE. AMEN.*

FIRST WEEK OF LENT

WEDNESDAY

RETURN TO THE LORD, YOUR
GOD, FOR HE IS GRACIOUS AND
MERCIFUL.

JOEL 2:13

A COVENANT
OF ETERNAL LOVE

In this past week, I have used the word *covenant* here and there, but today I would like to mention it specifically because it is the foundation upon which we rest and to which we continually return. If we allow the reality of covenant to inform our entire lives—mentally, emotionally, spiritually, physically, and sexually—we will live differently, for we will live in the truth of who we are.

God does not sign a contract with us. He makes a covenant with us. In very simple terms, a contract is an agreement of an exchange of goods, whereas a covenant is a pledge of an exchange of people—and the people who make the covenant do not give other people, but themselves and their descendants. A covenant says, "I am yours and you are mine." And with God it says, "I am yours and you are mine. Forever."

A covenant says, "I love you. I will never leave you. I will never forsake you. I am not going anywhere. I am here for you. No matter what happens, I will not reject you. I love you as you are, and I desire your ultimate good. I give myself to you completely and I receive you completely. You do not have to hide anything. You do not have to pretend. You can bring anything to me and I will be with you in it, bear it with you, and speak the truth to you about it in love." This is how God loves us. This is the freedom and responsibility of love.

We ache for this kind of love because this is the love in which we are made. We know this echo within our hearts, even if our tangible experiences of human love have been something much less (and we have all had these painful experiences). This covenant love is the pledge God makes to us, and he is the only one who can perfectly fulfill it.

He is yours and you are his.

REFLECT

What did you notice in your heart as you read through this reflection, especially regarding the characteristics of what covenant love says?

_____

_____

_____

_____

_____

_____

_____

_____

_____

_____

_____

PRAY

*GOD, FILL ME WITH YOUR LOVE.
INCREASE MY DESIRE TO BE
COMPLETELY OPEN TO YOU IN THIS
COVENANT OF ETERNAL LOVE. AMEN.*

FIRST WEEK OF LENT

THURSDAY

CREATE IN ME A CLEAN HEART,
O GOD . . . RESTORE TO ME THE
JOY OF YOUR SALVATION.

PSALM 51:10, 12

THE CAPTIVATING LOVE OF GOD

The covenant God makes with us is true and everlasting. It is not just a nice idea or a pious thought but an eternal reality that impacts us at every moment. For those of us who are baptized, this covenant is indelibly marked upon our souls. The covenant of the Sacrament of Baptism configures us to Christ; we belong to him. Jesus brings us into the same relationship that he has with the Father.

This truth roots us and grounds us in eternal love. This truth changes everything. It means that we are eternally marked as belonging to God as his beloved sons and daughters, and that he delights in us. It means that no matter what other people do to us or say to us, nothing can change this eternal reality of being eternally loved. It means we can have the subjective experiences of being betrayed, abused, abandoned, or rejected and feel the deep suffering of those experiences and still rest in the deepest reality that even if others leave us or forsake us, God never will. It means that whatever is happening in our lives right now is not the end of the story.

Even now as I write these words, the captivating love of God is so stunning to me. And this is why prayer is so foundational. Prayer heals our relationship with God, not on his end but ours.

Prayer is not mere words; prayer is life itself. This is why we pray without ceasing.

REFLECT

What are some areas of your life where you have need of being more rooted and grounded in the eternal truth of being the son or daughter of God?

_____

_____

_____

_____

_____

_____

_____

_____

_____

_____

_____

_____

_____

_____

_____

_____

_____

_____

_____

_____

_____

_____

_____

_____

_____

_____

_____

_____

_____

PRAY

_JESUS, ROOT ME AND GROUND ME
IN YOUR LOVE. MAY MY HEART REST
DEEPLY IN YOURS. AMEN._

FIRST WEEK OF LENT

FRIDAY

HAVE I ANY PLEASURE IN THE
DEATH OF THE WICKED, SAYS
THE LORD GOD, AND NOT
RATHER THAT HE SHOULD TURN
FROM HIS WAY AND LIVE?

EZEKIEL 18:23

OUR RESPONSE
TO HIS LOVE

As Adam and Eve are shattered in the garden by their decision to listen to the enemy and not to rely upon the truth of who God is, so are we. We hold God in suspicion, we blame him, we try to create our own reality apart from him, and we fear being seen by him. We fear being seen by the only one who can actually do anything to heal us.

God's response is to willingly suffer the effects of our choices, give us his very heart, and invite us into a covenant of love. The humility of God is staggering. How exquisite he is.

All caring relationships are built upon time and hearts shared together. We make time for those whom we love; what matters to them, matters to us. We care for them, and they for us. It is not always easy or fun, but we continue to go forward through it all.

When we spend time with God in prayer listening, receiving, speaking, pondering, and responding, our lives are changed. As we drink deeply from the scriptures and let this living Word settle into the marrow of our souls, the poison of sin and lies is drawn out. As we meditate and contemplate upon who God is and engage in conversation with him, our stony hearts are softened and made new. As we confess our sin and weaknesses and ask for his heart to meet us in our misery, new light dawns.

REFLECT

God's invitation into a covenant of love is continually made to each one of us at every moment. How will you respond today to this invitation from God?

_____

_____

_____

_____

_____

_____

_____

_____

_____

_____

_____

_____

_____

_____

_____

_____

_____

_____

_____

_____

_____

_____

_____

_____

_____

PRAY

*FATHER, HELP ME TO RESPOND
TO YOUR HEART FOR ME IN LOVE.
SOFTEN THE PLACES OF MY HEART
THAT ARE HARD AND CALLOUSED.
AMEN.*

FIRST WEEK OF LENT

SATURDAY

BLESSED ARE THOSE WHO KEEP
HIS TESTIMONIES, WHO SEEK
HIM WITH THEIR WHOLE HEART.

PSALM 119:2

LENT AS A
HEALING JOURNEY

We have spent a lot of time this past week and a half pondering who God is and what prayer, covenant, our heart, and love mean to us. This is on purpose. These truths will be the foundation upon which we will continue to build and, as we read earlier, continually return. The foundation matters the most.

A house may look lovely on the exterior, but if the foundation is flawed, the house will develop acute problems. We see this in our own lives: The Lord spends much time healing and restoring the roots of our lives. This happens little by little over time. Yes, we experience deep shifts and major breakthroughs within that are seismic and felt and lasting. And we also have tiny reverberations of the tender work of the Artist who knows exactly what he is creating.

Lent is a healing journey. Perhaps that is why Lent is so difficult at times. I often liken the human heart to a diamond: a diamond brilliantly sparkles in the light as the facets refract the light, and the human heart has many facets. We are not "all or nothing" but a mix of so many things.

Perhaps during these days you have already experienced the Lord illumining a facet of your heart, and you are saying to him, "This again!? I have already looked at this so many times." Yet there it is. As I see this happen many times in my own heart, I truly believe that this is God's way of integrating all the facets of our heart. God loves us so much that he will tirelessly visit every facet of our being to bring us into communion. He so gently and reverently comes to every fiber of our being that is isolated and fragmented to bring us into communion with him. He is the physician we have need of.

REFLECT

What areas of your life need healing? Do you experience mental, emotional, spiritual, physical, or sexual wounds? How might you give the Lord permission to come into any place of your life and bring you into wholeness and into relationship with himself?

_____

_____

_____

_____

_____

_____

_____

_____

_____

_____

_____

_____

_____

PRAY

*JESUS, PLEASE REVEAL AND HEAL ME
IN THESE PLACES. AMEN.*

PART 2

FASTING

HEALING OUR RELATIONSHIP WITH OURSELVES

PENITENTIAL FASTING IS OBVIOUSLY SOMETHING VERY DIFFERENT FROM A THERAPEUTIC DIET, BUT IN ITS OWN WAY IT CAN BE CONSIDERED THERAPY FOR THE SOUL. IN FACT, PRACTICED AS A SIGN OF CONVERSION, IT HELPS ONE IN THE INTERIOR EFFORT OF LISTENING TO GOD.

ST. JOHN PAUL II

SECOND WEEK
OF LENT

FREEDOM
OF HEART

SECOND WEEK OF LENT

SUNDAY

IT IS WELL THAT WE ARE HERE.

MARK 9:5

ORDERING OUR LOVES

We embark upon this second week of Lent taking the eternal love of God and prayer as the foundation of our lives. From this foundation, who we truly are emerges within the gaze of God. We find out who we truly are by being in relationship with God. Everything else flows from this source.

The second discipline that we practice during Lent is fasting. Fasting, in all of its forms, has many challenges and many benefits, but the main goal of fasting is freedom of heart and the ordering of our loves. Freedom of heart is gained by having mastery over our instincts but also by encountering our poverty and our incredible ache and need. Fasting orders our loves and desires. Its pang and pain remind us of what truly matters and how fragile we truly are.

Fasting is not shutting down our hearts or exercising self-reliance but rather opening our hearts to our deepest longings and having honest conversations with God about these places. This is a very good thing.

We all need to fast on a regular basis. A mix of fasting is also good for us. Unless one has a health condition, some form of food fasting is hugely beneficial. We can also fast from media, possessions, how we spend our time, the words we say. I would like to invite you to choose a few things to fast from and go deep with them. Spare the quantity for the quality and see what happens to you on this Lenten pilgrimage. Nothing is so difficult as saying no the next day to the things you feel inspired to fast from! And this is so good. For here the conversation begins.

REFLECT

What are your past experiences with fasting? Has it drawn you closer to the Lord, or do you need to reboot your understanding of it?

_____

_____

_____

_____

_____

_____

_____

_____

_____

_____

_____

_____

_____

_____

PRAY

*JESUS, GIVE ME THE COURAGE TO
SEE WHAT FASTING REVEALS IN MY
HEART. HELP ME TO KEEP GOING ON
THIS JOURNEY. AMEN.*

SECOND WEEK OF LENT

MONDAY

O GOD, WHO HAVE TAUGHT US
TO CHASTEN OUR BODIES
FOR THE HEALING OF OUR
SOULS,
ENABLE US, WE PRAY,
TO ABSTAIN FROM ALL SINS,
AND STRENGTHEN OUR HEARTS
TO CARRY OUT YOUR LOVING
COMMANDS.

COLLECT FOR MASS OF THE DAY

TURN TOWARD
THE LORD

As human beings, we are a union of body and soul. We are a profound union of spirit and matter. How we live spiritually affects us corporeally, and how we live corporeally affects us spiritually. When we do or don't do one thing in one area, it affects the other. The two go hand in hand. When we fast and allow that fasting to bring integration to our bodies, it also brings integration to our souls.

We see this in Genesis with Adam and Eve, before and after the Fall and the entrance of original sin. Before the rupture of sin, Adam and Eve experienced wholeness, communion, and integration of themselves with God, within themselves, with each other, and with creation. After the rupture of sin, this turning away from love, they experienced the disintegration of every aspect of their being.

Fasting helps reorder our loves so we can have the proper end in sight and live in true freedom. When our loves are out of order, our lives are out of order. Fasting helps reveal the places we need God's love the most and gives us the discipline to keep choosing him.

REFLECT

What are the areas in which you are inspired to fast this Lent?
How are they bringing you to freedom of heart?

_____

_____

_____

_____

_____

_____

_____

_____

_____

_____

_____

_____

_____

_____

_____

_____

_____

_____

_____

_____

_____

_____

_____

_____

_____

PRAY

*LORD, MAY MY FASTING THIS LENT
HELP ME TO CONTINUALLY TURN
TOWARD YOU. AMEN.*

SECOND WEEK OF LENT

TUESDAY

LIGHTEN MY EYES, LEST I SLEEP
THE SLEEP OF DEATH; LEST MY
ENEMY SAY, "I HAVE PREVAILED
OVER HIM."

PSALM 13:3

THE ACHE FOR COMMUNION

The earth that we live upon is not neutral territory. We live on not a cruise ship but a battlefield. And we know this battle through and through, as well as the ache for communion in eternal love.

A priest friend of mine, who is an exorcist, articulated this reality in sharp brilliance when he was sharing with me what he sees in the souls of people, their wounds, and their journey toward wholeness in Jesus.

These are his words: "After so many years of working with people and their deepest wounds, sins, and sorrows, I have come to realize a couple things about the nature of the battle we face on earth.

"First, our wounds are not arbitrary, they are not random. Satan is like a sniper. He intuits with his angelic intellect the destiny of every human person and he shoots his deadly arrows into the place that will do the most damage in order to thwart the flourishing of the person and God's plan for their life. Satan succeeds when he can convince us to hate God, hate ourselves, and hate others for the wounds we bear.

"Second, in God's mysterious and divine sovereignty, God allows Satan this access only to make the wounded places even more life-giving, beautiful, and glorious than they ever would have been otherwise, if we allow the restoration of these places. Even Satan's most vicious attacks are nothing in comparison to the immense sovereignty and love of God and the profound transformation that can take place."

I have pondered these two realities nearly every day since Father shared those insights. We will visit each of them in the coming days.

REFLECT

What are you noticing in your heart and mind as Father's insights are placed before you? What resonates within you?

_____

_____

_____

_____

_____

_____

_____

_____

_____

_____

_____

PRAY

GOD, THANK YOU FOR YOUR
SOVEREIGNTY. THANK YOU FOR
HOLDING EVERY MOMENT OF MY LIFE
IN YOUR HANDS AND THAT YOU MAKE
ALL THINGS NEW.

SECOND WEEK OF LENT

WEDNESDAY

DO NOT FORSAKE ME, O LORD!
O MY GOD, BE NOT FAR FROM
ME! MAKE HASTE TO HELP ME, O
LORD, MY SALVATION!

PSALM 38:21–22

THE PROBLEM
OF SUFFERING

Where have you experienced war being waged against you in your life? We all have these places—the places when we were little girls and little boys, even in the womb; the things that happened to us when we were twelve, eighteen, twenty-five years old, and older.

When these painful places rise to the surface of our heart, we usually try to avoid them, push them away, or find some distraction from their unwelcome intrusion. Or we try to minimize them and tell ourselves and others, "Get over it. It was a long time ago. Stop whining and get on with life. The past is the past; there is nothing that can be done about it." Yet their echoes remain.

There is a wonderful saying in healing circles that I find to be very true: "Suffering that is not transformed is transmitted." Every experience of suffering we have had that has not yet been redeemed and transformed by the love of Christ is transmitted to those around us. The suffering we have experienced does not just disappear; it is most often buried alive. And that pain buried alive continues to afflict us and those around us.

I know this may be very hard to admit to, dear friends, and I want to honor your hearts right here in this very moment. This process is not about digging up the past or blaming people but rather about allowing Jesus to gently bring to light the places in your heart he would like to tend to this Lenten season.

REFLECT

In the safety of where you are in this present moment, ask Jesus to reveal an area of your life he would like to particularly tend to during these days. He is with you. He goes before you. You are not alone.

_____

_____

_____

_____

_____

_____

_____

_____

_____

_____

_____

_____

PRAY

*HOLY SPIRIT, PLEASE ENLIGHTEN ME
AND COMFORT ME IN THIS PLACE OF
PAIN. PLEASE BRING YOUR PEACE AND
LIGHT. AMEN.*

SECOND WEEK OF LENT

THURSDAY

O GOD, WHO DELIGHT IN
INNOCENCE AND RESTORE
IT,
DIRECT THE HEARTS OF YOUR
SERVANTS TO YOURSELF.

COLLECT FOR MASS OF THE DAY

THE TRUTH OF
WHO YOU ARE

Holding very gently the place that has come to your heart these days, may I invite you to consider a few things surrounding that area of pain and suffering? I invite you to do this in as much as you feel safe to do so. Sometimes just a toe in the water is all we can do, and that is enough.

As you hold this place with Jesus before you, I would like to invite you to consider Father's words that Satan is like a sniper. Satan is the one who divides, scatters, shatters. He is the father of lies, and he is our enemy. He uses our brokenness, sinfulness, and weakness to inflict suffering upon ourselves and others, all in his waging war against God, a battle he has already lost.

In looking at this place in your heart, can you see how an enemy (often through the brokenness of ourselves or another) has done this? And as you behold this place of pain in your life, what are you honestly believing about yourself there? Many times we hold beliefs such as: "I am stupid. I am worthless. I have to be perfect to be loved. No one cares about me. I don't know what to do. I am dirty. I will never be well. I cannot trust anyone. I am not seen. I am not heard. I am all alone."

REFLECT

As you honestly bring those beliefs to Jesus here in this place, ask him to reveal the truth of who you are and his love for you here in this very place. What is happening within your heart, mind, and body as he speaks to you?

_____

_____

_____

_____

_____

_____

_____

_____

_____

_____

_____

_____

_____

_____

_____

_____

_____

_____

_____

_____

_____

_____

_____

PRAY

*JESUS, PLEASE REVEAL TO ME ANY
LIES I BELIEVE ABOUT MYSELF
BECAUSE OF THIS PLACE OF PAIN
AND SUFFERING. I RENOUNCE THESE
LIES IN YOUR NAME, JESUS, AND I
PROCLAIM THE TRUTH OF YOUR LOVE
FOR ME HERE. AMEN.*

SECOND WEEK OF LENT

FRIDAY

IN YOU, O LORD, I SEEK REFUGE,
LET ME NEVER BE PUT TO SHAME;
IN YOUR RIGHTEOUSNESS
DELIVER ME!

PSALM 31:1–2

OUR REFUGE

A refuge is a place where we are safe, where our hearts can rest, and where we find our home. God is our true and ultimate refuge, and the people he sends into our lives who love us authentically are emissaries of his safety and love.

As painful as life has been for us in moments, God is not our enemy. God is only good and offers goodness. He understands our pain and sorrow, our anger and rage. He is not afraid of it, disgusted by it, or deterred by it.

It is God who takes our sorrows and sufferings and makes them beautiful. As he rose from the dead with his open wounds in which we find refuge and restoration, so it is with us. Ultimately the places where we have been wounded are not death sentences but a sharing in Christ's own life, and he with us.

The enemy comes to steal, kill, and destroy. But Jesus comes that we might have life and have it more abundantly (see John 10:10). The abundant life means our hearts are fully alive in the grace of God. It means we experience the full range of our humanity in joy, sorrow, triumph, and tragedy. It means living as Jesus does in every way—fully open, fully human, fully loved.

REFLECT

As you continue to allow Jesus to bring the deep place of your heart to the fore, can you see, even if only in a glimpse, how Jesus is bringing you into communion in this place? Whereas this place of suffering may be one of isolation and shame for you, how can you experience the gentle presence of Jesus here, sitting beside you?

PRAY

*LORD, HELP ME TO SEE THAT THERE
IS A NEW WAY IN WHICH I CAN LIVE.
OPEN MY HEART TO SEE THE TRUTH.
AMEN.*

SECOND WEEK OF LENT

SATURDAY

O GOD, WHO GRANT US
   BY GLORIOUS HEALING
   REMEDIES WHILE STILL ON
   EARTH
TO BE PARTAKERS OF THE
   THINGS OF HEAVEN,
GUIDE US, WE PRAY, THROUGH
   THIS PRESENT LIFE
AND BRING US TO THAT LIGHT
   IN WHICH YOU DWELL.

COLLECT FOR MASS OF THE DAY

HIS LOVE
WASHES OVER US

The Lord gives us so many glorious healing remedies while still on earth. Yes, we will only know the fullness of wholeness and communion when we see God face-to-face in heaven, but that restoration begins to take place even now. The taste of that glory begins now.

As we sat with some deep places this week—perhaps new to us in revelation or long stories that we are quite familiar with—I want to allow those places to gently settle and unfold in the care of God.

Some time ago, I was pondering a similar place in my own heart. It was a place of poverty for me, one that came to the surface of my heart often and brought with it a mix of many emotions and thoughts. The first temptation of my heart was to become frustrated and discouraged at the seeming lack of healing there and the ongoing pain this part of my heart evoked when pressed upon in certain situations.

In his gentle kindness, the Lord revealed to me the image of a hand that was balled up into a fist. The fingers that curled over the palm of the hand were areas of self-protection, for at the center of the hand was an area of heartfelt pain. The fist was the self-protection and fear of opening up to the rawness of the sorrow's center.

The Lord then showed me gentle ocean waves that wash back and forth over the shore. These waves come in and they go out. Day after day, moment after moment, the waves wash upon the sand and rock, and slowly they change the shore—little by little.

This is the Lord's love for us. His love washes upon the shore of our hearts, gently cascading over these places of pain to tenderly open them and heal them.

Jesus is not interested in prying open our fists, nor in having us do so ourselves. He is not in a hurry. He gently loves us, and his love brings us the safety to open our fists over time so that his kindness can encounter the places of our pain.

Little by little and so gently, dear friends, we continue on our way.

REFLECT

What pain have you been protecting with your closed fist? How might you surrender this pain to Jesus today?

_____

_____

_____

_____

_____

_____

_____

_____

_____

_____

_____

_____

_____

_____

_____

_____

_____

_____

_____

_____

_____

_____

_____

PRAY

LORD, MAY YOUR GENTLE LOVE WASH
OVER THESE PLACES OF MY HEART.
AMEN.

THIRD WEEK
OF LENT

THE ROOTS
OF SIN

THIRD WEEK OF LENT

SUNDAY

I WILL SPRINKLE CLEAN WATER
UPON YOU, AND YOU SHALL
BE CLEAN FROM ALL YOUR
UNCLEANNESSES. . . . AND I
WILL PUT MY SPIRIT WITHIN YOU.

EZEKIEL 36:25, 27

THE ACHE OF EMPTINESS

You may be finding new areas of your heart that are tender and in need of God's kindness and truth. May I invite you to bring these areas to his heart as you pray, fast, and give alms?

In particular, what has been your experience of fasting so far this Lent? What happens within you as you experience the ache of the things you have surrendered for the season? If we look carefully within, we will often find a mix of things.

Sometimes we will notice that when we feel a hunger in one place, we will try to compensate for it in another place. Rather than sitting with the ache, we will compensate for it elsewhere in an attempt to alleviate the pain.

Elsewhere we might notice that when we feel the ache and emptiness that the object of our fasting filled, we will immediately give in to it. We promise ourselves that we can make up for it later and instead indulge now in the thing we chose to give up.

Or rather than indulge when we feel the ache, we will push away the ache and stoically push through the pang without engaging our heart, the deeper level of what our heart is saying to us, and what the aches are leading us to.

Our hearts are always trying to tell us something. And these clues lead us to the root places in our lives.

REFLECT

What are some of the tendencies you notice within yourself that fasting has revealed?

_____

_____

_____

_____

_____

_____

_____

_____

_____

_____

_____

_____

_____

_____

_____

_____

_____

_____

_____

_____

_____

_____

_____

_____

_____

_____

PRAY

*JESUS, MAY I HUNGER MORE DEEPLY
FOR YOU TODAY. MAY MY ACHES LEAD
ME TO CALL OUT TO YOU, SO YOU
CAN FILL ME. AMEN.*

THIRD WEEK OF LENT

MONDAY

MY SOUL LONGS, YES, FAINTS
FOR THE COURTS OF THE LORD;
MY HEART AND FLESH SING FOR
JOY TO THE LIVING GOD.

PSALM 84:2

THE ROOTS
OF OUR HUNGER

What are our aches trying to tell us? They tell us many things. Be it an ache for a certain kind of food, a particular person, a favorite pastime—our hearts are always speaking. Fasting calls to our attention that something far beyond ourselves is our ultimate fulfillment. Recall how we spent time earlier pondering how God orders our loves. Fasting is one of the ways he does this.

If we cannot say no to something, how can we really say yes to something? It really is amazing how difficult it can be to say no to the thing we have surrendered for Lent when it presents itself with such urgency. Suddenly that one thing can become all-encompassing, and we wonder what inspired us to give it up in the first place! It was probably the Lord, as he wishes us to bring our aches and hungers to him, so he can speak to us there. Our hearts and flesh cry out to and for the Lord.

When I fast from something and the ache comes to the fore, this is the exact place for conversation with the Lord. In the ache we come to him and admit our desire and longing and ask him to reveal the truth about our hungers and the places where we are using things or people in place of him.

When we exercise the muscle and virtue of fasting (temperance)—to behold the good of what we have surrendered, to allow the ache to surface, to bring our ache to the Lord and ask him to fill us, and to purify us, heal us, and strengthen us to be faithful—we grow. We grow in virtue, wholeness, integrity, love, and peace as we see our fragility and poverty, and we grow in our capacity as we allow God to order our loves. When we allow God to order our loves, first and foremost toward him, everything else becomes aligned.

REFLECT

Where is the place within that God wants to renew your spirit?
What is fasting revealing about the area in your life where you
need it the most?

_____

_____

_____

_____

_____

_____

_____

_____

_____

_____

_____

_____

_____

_____

_____

_____

_____

_____

_____

_____

_____

_____

_____

_____

PRAY

*LORD, HELP ME TO GROW IN VIRTUE,
ESPECIALLY WHEN IT IS MOST
DIFFICULT. AMEN.*

THIRD WEEK OF LENT

TUESDAY

MAY YOUR GRACE NOT
FORSAKE US, O LORD, WE
PRAY,
BUT MAKE US DEDICATED TO
YOUR HOLY SERVICE
AND AT ALL TIMES OBTAIN FOR
US YOUR HELP.

COLLECT FOR MASS OF THE DAY

FAST SO YOU
CAN FEAST

The priest who mentored me for many years before and after I entered religious life was very fond of offering the adage that when we fast from one thing, we need to feast on something else. This is not compensating for what we are aching for but offering our heart, mind, body, and soul the true food that it needs.

For example, when we fast from food, we feast on the Word of God. When we fast from media or movies, we feast on spending time in the presence of God and prayer. When we fast from busyness and hurry, we feast on being present to the present moment (and this becomes a way of life) and to the people God has placed before us.

Even sinful tendencies that we notice in ourselves can be avenues for deeper conversion. There is always a reason why we do what we do—as we said earlier, our hearts are always trying to tell us something. Many times we simply just try to "manage" the fruit of our sinful tree without ever looking more deeply into the roots of why we do what we do.

We will spend the next couple of days looking more closely at these areas and what they reveal, but for now, ask the Holy Spirit to enlighten you as to the areas of your life where the Lord wants to give you the true food.

REFLECT

What particular area is the Lord inviting you to feast upon today?

_____

_____

_____

_____

_____

_____

_____

_____

_____

_____

_____

_____

_____

_____

_____

_____

_____

_____

_____

_____

_____

_____

_____

_____

_____

_____

PRAY

*LORD, INCREASE MY AWARENESS
OF THE TRUE FOOD YOU ARE
CONSTANTLY OFFERING TO ME.
HELP ME TO SAY YES TO WHAT IS OF
ETERNAL VALUE. AMEN.*

THIRD WEEK OF LENT

WEDNESDAY

KEEP STEADY MY STEPS
ACCORDING TO YOUR PROMISE,
AND LET NO INIQUITY GET
DOMINION OVER ME.

PSALM 119:133

THE HIDDEN WAYS
OF OUR HEARTS

Jesus tells us that a tree is known by its fruit and that from the fullness of our heart, our mouth speaks (see Luke 6:43–45). Things can look really nice on the surface but underneath harbor darkness that inevitably manifests in certain ways sooner or later. I think this is why our words and our behavior surprise and befuddle us at times. We can be ardent about something in our words and yet behaviorally reveal the exact opposite. We have all said things that surprised us when they came out of our mouth, or in a moment of unguarded honesty, our words revealed what we truly believe or feel in our heart.

This is where real relationship exists—at the root of the tree. We can say all the nice and appropriate-sounding things in the world, but our behavior will reveal what we truly believe, and our emotions give us clues to the experience of our beliefs.

For true transformation to take place—the true ordering of our hearts and lives, interiorly and exteriorly—we must allow Jesus to come to the roots and bring his truth and love there. When we consider these places that manifest so painfully in our lives and in the lives of others, we frequently experience shame and wish to hide these places and ourselves. Or we seek to distract ourselves from them or blame someone else.

As Adam and Eve hid in the garden, so do we. In light of our story and where we hurt and how we try to avoid suffering, our sin and broken ways of living follow a pattern.

REFLECT

Today I invite you to ask the Holy Spirit to help you trace the trajectory of one of your repetitive sins or wounded ways of relating. With the Holy Spirit, ask for illumination as to the following questions:

1. What happened? What did you do or how did you react to a certain person or situation?
2. What were you feeling at the time? (Be very honest.)
3. What were you believing about yourself?

Sit with the Lord in these places and just notice what arises in your heart and what he says to you there.

_____

_____

_____

_____

_____

_____

_____

_____

_____

_____

PRAY

COME, HOLY SPIRIT, REVEAL TO ME
THE HIDDEN WAYS OF MY HEART.
AMEN.

THIRD WEEK OF LENT

THURSDAY

I AM THE SALVATION OF THE
PEOPLE, SAYS THE LORD.
SHOULD THEY CRY TO ME IN
ANY DISTRESS,
I WILL HEAR THEM AND I WILL
BE THEIR LORD FOR EVER.

**ENTRANCE ANTIPHON FOR MASS
OF THE DAY**

WHAT SIN REVEALS

Perhaps one of the most frustrating and sorrowful experiences we have as human beings is when another person doesn't understand us or doesn't "get" us. It's a tiring thing at times to continually try to explain ourselves or hope that somehow someone can just intuit and fully experience what we are experiencing on the inside. Perhaps we have all wished that someone would just fully "know" our heart, know our internal landscape, and attend to us there. It's painful to share our heart or face our broken places and not be met there by another who can understand. Contrarily, when someone does understand our heart and is a safe presence of love, our heart feels received and we can rest and breathe.

The Lord has placed people in our lives who know us and love us and can understand us to varying degrees, but the Lord is the only one who knows and loves us and understands us fully. God knows us better than we know ourselves, and he receives us completely and continually. God does not reject even the places that we reject within ourselves. He is captivating in his goodness, attentiveness, and gentleness.

REFLECT

What is the Lord revealing to you in this pattern of your sin? What needs are you trying to satisfy or what suffering are you trying to avoid?

As you explore the situation of what you did or how you reacted, does what you were feeling and believing about yourself there feel familiar to you? And the things that feel familiar to you—are there any memories attached to them that the Lord would like to bring to the surface?

I will give you an example of all of these components in the coming days, but for now, see what the Lord brings to your heart and mind. He knows you, he understands you, and he delights to bring your heart into communion in this very place.

PRAY

JESUS, YOU KNOW ME BETTER THAN I KNOW MYSELF. YOU COMPLETELY UNDERSTAND ME. HELP ME TO SEE MYSELF AS YOU SEE ME. AMEN.

THIRD WEEK OF LENT

FRIDAY

POUR YOUR GRACE INTO OUR
HEARTS, WE PRAY, O LORD,
THAT WE MAY BE CONSTANTLY
DRAWN AWAY FROM UNRULY
DESIRES
AND OBEY BY YOUR OWN GIFT
THE HEAVENLY TEACHING
YOU GIVE US.

COLLECT FOR MASS OF THE DAY

THE NATURE OF DESIRE

Bob Schuchts, founder of the John Paul II Healing Center and the author of several books including *Be Healed* and *Be Restored*, explains our unruly desires like this: "Behind every disordered desire is a good and holy desire, an unmet need, an unhealed wound, and a hidden pattern of sin."

We commonly get stuck at the level of "disordered desire," and as we mentioned earlier, we try to manage that desire or the sin without exploring with the Lord the deeper roots. Christianity is not about sin management or mere behavior modification but rather a complete transformation unto glory. Christ came to help us with these places and to heal of our sin and division. He came to bring us into his own divine life.

So let's look at these components of what is happening in our heart. We have been pondering lately the action, the sin, the disordered desire we have. We have been asking the Lord to reveal to us what we were feeling and believing because this helps reveal what our good and holy desire is.

For example, maybe you struggle with gossip. There are many roots as to why we gossip, but let's look at what can be happening in your heart when you choose to gossip.

The disordered desire/action here is the gossip itself. What is the good and holy desire underneath it? Perhaps you wanted to feel included or that you belong to a group and are accepted there. Or maybe you are angry with that person because they hurt you and it seemed easier to gossip about them rather than face the pain with your heart or speak to them personally. Or maybe you are jealous of that person and so undermining them seems to take away some of the sting of that ache in your heart as you behold their life that seems so beautiful and unlike yours.

The desires to be in communion with others, to feel included, to belong, to have restoration when we are hurting in our hearts and to have beautiful things in our lives are good desires. These deeper desires can be painful to admit.

REFLECT

What is the good and holy desire beneath your disordered desire or action?

\
\
\
\
\
\
\
\
\
\
\
\
\
\

_____

_____

_____

_____

_____

_____

_____

_____

_____

_____

PRAY

*LORD, INCREASE THE GOOD AND
HOLY DESIRES THAT YOU HAVE GIVEN
ME. GIVE ME THE WILLINGNESS TO
BRING EVERY DISORDERED DESIRE
TO YOU SO THAT YOU CAN HEAL IT.
AMEN.*

THIRD WEEK OF LENT

SATURDAY

FOR YOU TAKE NO DELIGHT
IN SACRIFICE; WERE I TO GIVE
YOU A BURNT OFFERING, YOU
WOULD NOT BE PLEASED. THE
SACRIFICE ACCEPTABLE TO GOD
IS A BROKEN SPIRIT; A BROKEN
AND CONTRITE HEART, O GOD,
YOU WILL NOT DESPISE.

PSALM 51:16–17

UNHEALED WOUNDS

Taking another step on our journey to the roots of our repetitive sin and wounded ways of relating, what is the unmet need and the unhealed wound underlying our sin?

Continuing to use our example of gossip—maybe in our life there is an unmet need of communion and belonging with others. Maybe we feel that no one in our life listens to us or really hears our heart and takes us seriously with attentiveness and love. Maybe we don't feel as though we have a safe place to bring our sorrows, and we have had to bury our anger our entire life.

Maybe we have wounds of rejection, abandonment, shame, fear, powerlessness, hopelessness, or confusion. These unhealed wounds and unacknowledged needs (that often tie back to our childhoods with long histories and patterns) continue to play out over and over again in our lives. Collectively they are the proverbial "iceberg under the water" that drives so much of our painful behavior.

What we begin to see is that sin is not "random." Nothing we do is random. The hidden pattern of sin behind our disordered desires/actions can be judgments of other people, unforgiveness, resentment, self-reliance, or an array of things that keep the painful wounds and unmet needs active and open.

You may be tempted to close the book now and walk away from this journey with the Lord. It may feel overwhelming or you may feel relieved to finally have some divine light shed upon a repetitive pattern in your life.

Whatever it may be, I would like to invite you to remember that the Lord does not reveal anything he does not also wish to heal.

If we want to be well, these are the places we must allow the Lord to gently lead us.

REFLECT

What is happening in your heart as you explore these places with the Lord?

_____

_____

_____

_____

_____

_____

_____

_____

_____

_____

_____

_____

_____

_____

_____

_____

_____

_____

_____

_____

_____

_____

_____

PRAY

*JESUS, YOU ARE WITH ME. YOU GO
BEFORE ME. YOU LOVE ME. I AM NOT
ALONE. AMEN.*

PART 3
ALMSGIVING

HEALING OUR RELATIONSHIP WITH OTHERS

NO ONE HEALS HIMSELF BY WOUNDING ANOTHER.

ST. AMBROSE

FOURTH WEEK OF LENT

THE HEALING BALM OF ALMSGIVING

FOURTH WEEK OF LENT

SUNDAY

SON, YOU ARE ALWAYS WITH ME,
AND ALL THAT IS MINE IS YOURS.

LUKE 15:31

WE BELONG TO
EACH OTHER

We take everything we have journeyed with during these weeks and continue to allow it to unfold as we embrace the third discipline of almsgiving. Almsgiving heals our relationships with others. Almsgiving can be defined as material or financial help given to those in need. It is an act of charity, an act of love, a work of mercy, and a restoration of our hearts. It is a healing balm for it invites us to go beyond ourselves to be with another. Almsgiving also takes many other forms.

Far from just a dissociated act of "giving" and then going on our way, almsgiving is love, or our desire to be shaped by love, which makes it a transformative experience. It is a gift of the heart. It is an act of communion. As Christ is deeply moved at the sight of the needs of the crowds (see Matthew 9:36, 14:14, and Mark 6:34), our need to give alms draws us into his relationship of communion.

Almsgiving is a recognition that all of us have needs, all of us are poor in some way or another, and none of us exists alone and isolated. Others in life have need of what we can give them, and we have need of what others can give us. To give something brings us out of ourselves into a deep recognition of the other. It heals us and the other person as well.

Giving alms frees us from narrow-mindedness, stinginess, and disordered attachment to things. It brings about the realization that we belong to each other. We need it. Oh, how we need it. It can often be penitential because it cuts us at our deepest level of selfishness and self-centeredness. The world is not all about us. The other serves as a constant reminder that we are made for communion and relationship.

REFLECT

What are the honest thoughts that arise in your heart as you ponder almsgiving? What do you experience within as you think about really making a gift of yourself to someone else?

_____

_____

_____

_____

_____

_____

_____

_____

_____

_____

_____

_____

_____

PRAY

*LORD, PLEASE OPEN MY EYES SO I
CAN SEE AS YOU SEE, THE ONE RIGHT
BEFORE ME, WHO HAS DEEP NEED.
OPEN MY HEART TO BRING ME INTO
COMMUNION WITH THEM AND WITH
YOU. AMEN.*

FOURTH WEEK OF LENT

MONDAY

JESUS SAID TO HIM, "GO; YOUR
SON WILL LIVE."

JOHN 4:50

A PIERCED HEART FOR
THE SAKE OF THE OTHER

Jesus does not refuse those who come to him and ask in their need. He never refuses an earnest prayer of the heart. Although the way he answers our needs and prayers may be different from what we anticipate, Jesus always gives to us from his heart.

We see throughout the gospels the different ways that Jesus ministers to what is needed in the cries of our hearts and lives, and no one leaves the presence of Christ without an encounter of his goodness and truth. Stomachs are fed, the dead are raised, the sick are healed, sins are forgiven, the proud are admonished, and the lamp of the heart and mind is illumined. Jesus does the same with us and invites us into communion in these very places.

Jesus invites us to do the same with others. The Sermon on the Mount (see Matthew 5–7) provides us with prolific instruction and invitation to the fullness (perfection) of living that begins now and finds its fulfillment in eternity. It is the law of the new covenant and the source of countless commentaries and reflections. Suffice it here to say that it bears great beauty for our reflection these last two weeks of Lent before Holy Week. For in it Jesus reveals to us the path on which we must walk.

Like prayer and fasting, almsgiving can take many forms, which we will encounter in these days. Today, though, is there someone in your life or someone you may see on a street corner as you drive about your day that you need to give assistance to? Can you give a bottle of water, some food, a gift card, or some other material support to them? Is there a crisis pregnancy center in town that needs donations of diapers or baby formula? There are so many ways for us to materially help others today. Can you "pay it forward" somewhere today where you will be?

REFLECT

What is one concrete way you can give alms today?

_____

_____

_____

_____

_____

_____

_____

_____

_____

_____

_____

_____

_____

_____

_____

_____

_____

_____

_____

_____

_____

_____

_____

_____

_____

_____

PRAY

JESUS, HELP ME TO RESPOND TO THE NEEDY YOU BRING INTO MY LIFE. ALLOW SORROW FOR THEIR SUFFERING TO PIERCE MY HEART, AND HELP ME BE GENEROUS WITH MATERIAL ASSISTANCE. AMEN.

FOURTH WEEK OF LENT

TUESDAY

DO YOU WANT TO BE HEALED?

JOHN 5:6

DO YOU WANT TO BE WELL?

This question above from the Gospel of John always pierces me. Jesus continually comes to us where we are ill and in need and asks us if we want to be well. As we recall our Lenten journey thus far, we know that if we are honest, we all have places in our lives where we are not well, where we are out of communion and experiencing isolation, and where we need healing. And as we discover, it is through communion that healing gushes forth.

Through an encounter, communion, with himself, Jesus heals a man who had been sick for a very long time. True communion with Jesus brings healing. Jesus comes to inquire about a willingness to be well, speaks the truth to the man, heals him of his sickness and sin, and sets the man free. Jesus helps the man and restores him beyond measure. This is what love does.

But love has to be present to heal. Love is what heals. The true presence of another brings healing. How often we can be physically with someone but not truly present to them. Our mind and emotions can be somewhere else, or we can be with someone but not receiving them as they are, for who they are.

One of the best ways we can give alms is to give our presence and undivided attention to another. How hard this can be! It is frequently so difficult just to sit with someone and be with them—to truly listen and receive them without getting distracted or try to fix them, save them, or give unsolicited advice.

And yet this is often the very thing we want the most—to be seen, received, and loved. Jesus is truly present to us and receives us.

REFLECT

What do you notice within you as you practice being truly present to others today, allowing Christ's heart to love through you?

PRAY

JESUS, REVEAL YOUR HEART TO ME
AND HOW YOU LOVE EACH PERSON
IN MY LIFE. TEACH ME HOW TO LOVE
THEM AND BE PRESENT TO THEM AS
YOU ARE TO ME. AMEN.

FOURTH WEEK OF LENT

WEDNESDAY

BUT ZION SAID, "THE LORD
HAS FORSAKEN ME, MY LORD
HAS FORGOTTEN ME." "CAN A
WOMAN FORGET HER SUCKLING
CHILD, THAT SHE SHOULD HAVE
NO COMPASSION ON THE SON
OF HER WOMB? EVEN THESE MAY
FORGET, YET I WILL NOT FORGET
YOU."

ISAIAH 49:14–15

THE GIFT OF TENDERNESS

What does the word and connotation of *tenderness* evoke for you? It can stir many things. Tenderness pierces us. It disarms us. It can also arouse fear and intense longing for safety and refuge. The gentleness, compassion, and kindness of tenderness is a language like no other. It is the currency of restoration and the heart becoming fully alive. It is fierce. It is life-giving.

Although there is a time and place for the entire range of appropriate responses to the needs of another, there is a particular power of tenderness that ministers to the deep places of every heart and soul. Jesus is stunning in his beauty and tenderness to the woman caught in adultery (see John 8:2–11), to the woman at the well (see John 4:1–42), and to Peter after his betrayal (see John 21:1–19). The tenderness of Jesus is fierce, honest, and captivating. His tenderness evokes repentance, conversion, and love (see Romans 2:4).

Tenderness is not weakness or shying away from the hard things. Tenderness is the very thing that makes hard things palatable, for it is the truth spoken and lived in love. We have all had moments when we were covered in shame and self-hatred, and the tenderness and compassion (to suffer with) of another broke our façade and the ache for love and the cry for life spilled out. Such richness, this tenderness. We all yearn for it.

REFLECT

How will you give this gift today?

_____

_____

_____

_____

_____

_____

_____

_____

_____

_____

_____

_____

PRAY

*JESUS, PLEASE BRING TO MY HEART
AND MIND THE PERSON WHO NEEDS
THE ALMS OF MY TENDERNESS THE
MOST. AMEN.*

FOURTH WEEK OF LENT

THURSDAY

WE EVOKE YOUR MERCY IN
HUMBLE PRAYER, O LORD,
THAT YOU MAY CAUSE US,
YOUR SERVANTS,
CORRECTED BY PENANCE
AND SCHOOLED BY GOOD
WORKS,
TO PERSEVERE SINCERELY IN
YOUR COMMANDS
AND COME SAFELY TO THE
PASCHAL FESTIVITIES.

COLLECT FOR MASS OF THE DAY

LOVE IN ACTION

Love is made concrete in action. We believe love when the utterance becomes lived. Jesus comes among us as one who loves, the one who is love, and the one who serves. He speaks of this reality and shows us in so many ways (see Mark 10:45 and John 13:1–17). Service manifests love, and these good works strengthen the bond of love and heal our selfish tendencies.

Traditionally in the Catholic Church, we speak of the corporeal and spiritual works of mercy. Both are love in action. The corporeal works of mercy—feed the hungry, give drink to the thirsty, shelter the homeless, visit the sick, visit the imprisoned, bury the dead, and give alms to the poor (all gleaned from Matthew 25:31–46)—meet the physical needs of those around us and in the world. They are tangible actions of relieving the misery of another.

Jesus is so serious about these acts of service and works of mercy that he equates them (or the lack of doing them) with his very self as he says, "Truly, I say to you, as you did it to one of the least of these my brethren, you did it to me" (Mt 25:40). Almsgiving brings communion, and the lack thereof breaks communion. Jesus reveals to us time and time again how love must be poured out in action, with his ultimate act being the gift of his very self on the Cross for us. Jesus speaks of his love for creation and then shows it, and we must do the same. Love costs everything. And it is worth it.

REFLECT

How will you come to serve, not to be served, today?

_____

_____

_____

_____

_____

_____

_____

_____

_____

_____

_____

PRAY

*JESUS, THANK YOU FOR SHOWING ME
HOW TO POUR OUT LOVE IN SERVICE.
PLEASE HELP ME TO MAKE A GIFT OF
MYSELF TODAY. AMEN.*

FOURTH WEEK OF LENT

FRIDAY

GRANT, WE PRAY, O LORD,
THAT, AS WE PASS FROM OLD
TO NEW,
SO, WITH FORMER WAYS LEFT
BEHIND,
WE MAY BE RENEWED IN
HOLINESS OF MIND.

PRAYER AFTER COMMUNION

THE SPIRITUAL
WORKS OF MERCY

As we practice the corporeal works of mercy, so we also practice the spiritual works of mercy. These works attend to the spiritual needs of those around us. Although perhaps not as widely known or exercised as the corporeal works of mercy, these works are just as needed.

The spiritual works of mercy: counseling the doubtful, instructing the ignorant, admonishing the sinner, comforting the sorrowful, forgiving injuries, bearing wrongs patiently, and praying for the living and the dead.

As you read the list, you will probably find certain ones easier (and more palatable!) than others. We will spend next week delving into forgiving injuries, but for now, I would like to invite you to ponder the realities of admonishing the sinner and bearing wrongs patiently. I chose these two spiritual works of mercy because they are typically challenging and many times misunderstood, but they lead to great growth in our lives and the lives of others.

What does it mean to "admonish" a sinner? Perhaps the thought can make our stomachs turn with the fear of confrontation or the threat of rejection. Or perhaps we think it means that we must judge and revile someone or harshly accost them for their wayward choices. We cringe at the times someone has done these things to us.

To admonish someone for their sins is something much different. It means to humbly and firmly warn, advise, or urge someone earnestly. It requires us to be very honest and forthright about our own lives, taking the log out of our own eye so we can see clearly to take the speck out of the other's eye (see Matthew 7:1–5). It means critically discerning with prayer and asking the Holy Spirit to open that person's heart and the timing of the encounter and to fill us with love and truth so that we can, when needed, humbly offer someone the gift of life and light.

We offer the gift and surrender the rest to God, asking him to make up for any defect and to order that person's heart and ours as well. And then we pray (and even offer fasting) for that person.

REFLECT

Who needs this gift of alms from you?

_____

_____

_____

_____

_____

_____

_____

_____

_____

_____

_____

_____

_____

_____

_____

_____

_____

_____

_____

_____

_____

_____

PRAY

_HOLY SPIRIT, FILL MY HEART AND
ORDER MY LIFE. GROUND ME IN
YOUR TRUTH AND LOVE AND GIVE ME
THE COURAGE TO SPEAK THE TRUTH
TO OTHERS WHEN YOU ASK ME TO.
AMEN._

FOURTH WEEK OF LENT

SATURDAY

THE SNARES OF DEATH
ENCOMPASSED ME; THE PANGS
OF SHEOL LAID HOLD ON ME;
I SUFFERED DISTRESS AND
ANGUISH. THEN I CALLED ON
THE NAME OF THE LORD: "O
LORD, I BEG YOU, SAVE MY LIFE!"

PSALM 116:3–4

BEARING WRONGS
WITH PATIENCE

Most of the painful situations we face as human beings have to do with the wrongs that others do to us. Remember the phrase we pondered from week 2: "Suffering that is not transformed is transmitted." It is incredibly difficult and heart-wrenching when we are hurt by others, and it is especially excruciating when the suffering is unjust and unwarranted.

We have a variety of ways of coping when it comes to bearing wrongs. Sometimes we shut down, numb ourselves, and shut off our hearts to protect ourselves from further pain. Other times we become self-righteous, judgmental, bitter, and vengeful to protect ourselves from further pain. We just want the pain to stop, and the anguish is so great that we will do whatever seems to mitigate against the sorrow.

The bearing of wrongs, not with bitterness or numbness but with patience, is a great and crucifying gift. It means that there is a real way to freedom and restoration through suffering and the wrongs that others inflict upon us. It means that there is resurrection even in experiences of death.

Patience speaks of the heart opening, enduring, offering, grieving, and loving. It is Jesus on the Cross. It is the whisper of agony to God when no one else knows or understands the depths or length or breadth of our hearts. It is the fruit of the Holy Spirit who gives us the capacity and fortitude to keep going with our faces fixed on God, receiving the grace of his love, newness, and communion even in the difficulty.

It is bearing wrongs, not with denial or vindictiveness but with patience, that can convert the hardened heart—our own heart and the heart of the one who has hurt us.

REFLECT

What is an area of your life where you have been bearing a wrong with numbness, bitterness, or another coping mechanism? What would you like Jesus to know about this part of your heart? What would you like to ask him for?

_____

_____

_____

_____

_____

_____

_____

_____

PRAY

*JESUS, I OFFER YOU MY HEART
AND THE PLACES WHERE BEARING
WRONGS FROM OTHER PEOPLE HAS
BEEN SO DIFFICULT. PLEASE FORGIVE
ME FOR THE WAYS I HAVE TRIED TO
DESTRUCTIVELY COPE AND SAVE
MYSELF AND TURN AWAY FROM YOUR
LOVE. PLEASE BE WITH ME HERE AND
GIVE ME THE GIFT OF TRUE PATIENCE
WITH AN OPEN AND OFFERING HEART,
UNITED TO YOU. AMEN.*

FIFTH WEEK
OF LENT

THE JOURNEY
OF
FORGIVENESS

FIFTH WEEK OF LENT

SUNDAY

AND JESUS SAID, "NEITHER DO
I CONDEMN YOU; GO, AND DO
NOT SIN AGAIN."

JOHN 8:11

RECEIVING FORGIVENESS

If almsgiving is a restoration of our hearts and a healing means of communion between persons, then at the heart of that reality would be the forgiveness of one another. Even mentioning the word *forgiveness* might conjure up old situations that are unresolved or desires for healing relationships that are ever present. Whatever our personal experience with forgiveness or the lack thereof, Jesus wants to meet us in this very place and bring our hearts to freedom.

Forgiveness is so important that when the disciples ask Jesus how they are to pray, he instructs them by embedding this truth in the prayer we know as the Lord's Prayer (see Matthew 6:9–13 and Luke 11:1–4). Not only does Jesus exhort us to ask the Father to "forgive us our trespasses, as we forgive those who trespass against us," but also he immediately reiterates and augments this portion of the prayer at its conclusion to expound upon the necessity of it (see Matthew 6:14–15). Of all the things Jesus could beseech us to pray for and about, he insists upon forgiveness. But he does not just speak about it; he shows us the reality of it upon the Cross, offering his life on behalf of the forgiveness of our sins, pleading with the Father to "forgive them; for they know not what they do" (Lk 23:34).

Yet forgiving others and ourselves is at times the most difficult thing for us to do. Unforgiveness stands in the way of much of our healing and restoration, freedom and wholeness. The journey of forgiveness is a process that we will explore this week in an intimate way. Jesus goes before you here. Will you follow him in whatever he wants to reveal to your heart?

REFLECT

What has been your experience of receiving forgiveness from God and others? Ask the Holy Spirit to bring to your mind a tangible experience you had of being forgiven and set free.

_____

_____

_____

_____

_____

_____

_____

_____

_____

PRAY

*JESUS, PLEASE TAKE MY HAND AS
I GO WITH YOU INTO THIS AREA
OF MY HEART AND LIFE WHERE I
NEED TO BE FORGIVEN AND WHERE
I NEED TO FORGIVE OTHERS WHO
HAVE HURT ME. GIVE ME THE
COURAGE, STRENGTH, AND SAFETY
TO WELCOME YOUR HEALING POWER
INTO MY HEART AND ALLOW YOU TO
TRANSFORM MY LIFE. AMEN.*

FIFTH WEEK OF LENT

MONDAY

EVEN THOUGH I WALK THROUGH
THE VALLEY OF THE SHADOW OF
DEATH, I FEAR NO EVIL; FOR YOU
ARE WITH ME.

PSALM 23:4

HONORING
OUR EMOTIONS

What about forgiveness makes it feel so insurmountable at times? Why are there some things that are relatively easy to forgive and other things that continue to be sources of pain, anger, and powerlessness for years on end? And why would Jesus ask us to do something that seems impossible at times?

Although there are no easy answers to any of these questions, we can begin to understand that our hearts are always trying to tell us something. Our emotions often reveal to us what we truly believe about a situation, whether we want to admit to it intellectually or not. Our emotions may not always be rational in proportion to a given experience, but they are very important messengers of the things we hold truest within our lived experience in what we believe about God, ourselves, others, and life.

We need not revel in our emotions, nor do we need to let them remain hidden outside the healing light of Christ. Our emotions, in their essence, are given to us by God to move us toward what is good and away from what is evil. They must be brought out into the light, felt, and acknowledged; then we can choose with the wisdom of Christ what is the best course of action.

REFLECT

When you think about a certain person who has hurt you, what emotions rise to the surface? Can you name the emotions honestly for what they are? As you do this, you will most likely experience a physical reaction somewhere in your body relating to the emotions evoked. Just notice what happens. Can you ask Jesus to be with you here and reveal to you what he wants you to know?

_____

_____

_____

_____

_____

_____

_____

_____

_____

_____

_____

_____

_____

_____

_____

_____

_____

_____

_____

_____

_____

_____

_____

PRAY

*JESUS, PLEASE HELP ME ALLOW
MY EMOTIONS TO SURFACE IN THE
SAFETY OF YOUR LOVE AND WISDOM.
PLEASE HEAL MY EMOTIONS IN BOTH
EXCESS AND DEFECT. HELP ME TO
LIVE FULLY ALIVE IN YOUR LOVE.
AMEN.*

FIFTH WEEK OF LENT

TUESDAY

HEAR MY PRAYER, O LORD; LET
MY CRY COME TO YOU!

PSALM 102:1

ENGAGING THE HEART

As we encounter the emotions that arise from the suffering we experience, we notice that emotions and our thoughts before and afterward are always in response to some*thing*. Our emotions and thoughts are not arbitrary. Contrary to what we may say and feel at times, our thoughts and emotions do not come out of nowhere. They are always evoked by some event.

Let us gently press into this area of the person who hurt you. The emotions you experience have to do with something that person did (or did not do). We may say something like, "I am so mad at them." But the anger is about something that happened, something that person did or failed to do, some way they failed to love us.

The degree of pain we experience has much to do with the event that happened and how close (either emotionally or physically) that person is to us, but forgiveness has to do with the things that happened. We cannot generically forgive someone. Forgiveness involves taking an honest account of what they actually unjustly did to us or took from us and how they hurt us.

And this is the difficult part. Forgiveness requires an engagement of our heart. It is not words alone. This engagement often takes time, and it comes in layers and stages, but this is the way through to true freedom.

REFLECT

May I invite you to take a deep breath? Would you be willing today to take an honest account of what that person did to you and how it hurt you? Allow whatever is in your heart and mind to surface. You are not alone. Jesus is with you. You are loved.

PRAY

*HOLY SPIRIT, PLEASE ILLUMINE MY
HEART AND MIND IN THE PLACES I
NEED IT THE MOST. AMEN.*

FIFTH WEEK OF LENT

WEDNESDAY

AND YOU WILL KNOW THE
TRUTH, AND THE TRUTH WILL
MAKE YOU FREE.

JOHN 8:32

HEALING THROUGH FORGIVENESS

The process of naming the areas of hurt that have kept us bound and captive to darkness is very important. Underneath the anger we experience (which in its pure form is a positive emotion to help us right what is wrong) is much sorrow and grief. If we cannot face this sorrow, grief, anger, and truth of what happened and allow it to be expressed in a healthy manner, it will go underground within us and tend to manifest in other ways through unhealthy expressions such as resentment, bitterness, addiction, revenge, criticism, grudges, self-hatred and hatred of the other, gossip, self-righteousness, judgment, contempt, and shame—just to name a few. From this pain comes many of the lies we believe about ourselves. Our identity is slowly outsourced to untruths, embedded survival mechanisms, and the passing opinion of others.

If we want to be well, dear friends, we must be continually honest down to the roots. St. Ambrose is quoted as saying, "We will never heal ourselves by wounding another." And how true this is. As in the parable of the unforgiving servant (see Matthew 18:21–35), we interiorly seize the person who hurt us, and we choke and throttle them, demanding they pay back what they owe us.

But how can they? How can a parent pay you back for the times they dismissed your heart, pushed you away, or chose another sibling over you? How can the kids in fifth grade pay you back for bullying you, calling you horrendous names, and excluding you from the lifeblood of friendship? How can your spouse pay you back for withholding love, being unfaithful, or being just too distracted to really see you and receive you?

So what are we to do? Herein lies the quandary.

Jesus shows us another way, the true way. It is through forgiveness that these wounds are tended to and brought into healing. This is the way.

REFLECT

Where have you been trying to heal yourself by wounding another?

_____

_____

_____

_____

_____

_____

_____

_____

_____

_____

_____

_____

_____

_____

_____

_____

_____

_____

_____

_____

_____

_____

_____

_____

PRAY

LORD, PLEASE HELP ME TO SEE.
AMEN.

FIFTH WEEK OF LENT

THURSDAY

O THAT TODAY YOU WOULD
LISTEN TO HIS VOICE!
HARDEN NOT YOUR HEARTS.

PSALM 95:7–8

CHOOSING TO FORGIVE

"Now—and this is daunting—this outpouring of mercy cannot penetrate our hearts as long as we have not forgiven those who have trespassed against us. Love, like the Body of Christ, is indivisible; we cannot love the God we cannot see if we do not love the brother or sister we do see. In refusing to forgive our brothers and sisters, our hearts are closed and their hardness makes them impervious to the Father's merciful love; but in confessing our sins, our hearts are opened to his grace" (CCC 2840).

None of us ultimately wants to live with a hard heart. We might do so, even unknowingly, because we have become used to living that way as an avenue to protect ourselves, but I do not believe this is what we truly want or deeply desire.

Forgiveness is not letting someone off the hook. It is not saying that what happened to us did not matter. It is not words alone. It is not pretending things are fine. It is not condoning bad behavior. It is not skipping justice. All of these things keep our hearts hard, in denial, and in the cycle of pain and resentment.

Forgiveness is asking Jesus Christ for the grace to forgive. It is relinquishing our grasp upon the person who hurt us, surrendering the person to Jesus and asking Jesus to restore justice. It is an acknowledgment of the pain inflicted, how it affected us, an ongoing emotional release of it, and a decision to offer that person and ourselves a gift of love and freedom.

Forgiveness is choosing to no longer seek revenge, be at war with that person, or try to save ourselves. Forgiveness is accepting the sorrow and grief and allowing Jesus to bring us through these places and into the Resurrection, into new life.

Jesus offers us this grace and this gift from his very self.

REFLECT

How might you become willing to receive this gift, even in one small step today?

_____

_____

_____

_____

_____

_____

_____

_____

_____

_____

_____

_____

_____

_____

_____

_____

_____

_____

_____

_____

_____

_____

_____

_____

PRAY

_JESUS, HELP ME TO FORGIVE THE
PERSON WHO HURT ME, EVEN IF IT'S
ONLY IN ONE SMALL STEP. I NEED
YOUR GRACE AND YOUR LOVE HERE.
LORD, I NEED YOU._

FIFTH WEEK OF LENT

FRIDAY

THE WORDS THAT I HAVE SPOKEN
TO YOU ARE SPIRIT AND LIFE.
. . . YOU HAVE THE WORDS OF
ETERNAL LIFE.

JOHN 6:63, 68

A FORGIVENESS MEDITATION

I would like to offer a forgiveness meditation for you today. Find a comfortable and quiet place and ask the Holy Spirit to lead you through these steps. You can pray this meditation as many times as needed and for as long as it takes. Certain wounds take a long time to heal, and that is okay.

1. Ask the Holy Spirit to show you whom you need to forgive. (It could be a family member, a friend, an abuser, or yourself.)
2. Picture the person in front of you and pay attention to what you feel in your heart and body.
3. Make an account of the debt they owe you. (What did they take from you? How did they hurt you? It is okay to feel angry or nothing at all.)
4. Imagine telling them what they did to hurt you and how it has affected you.
5. Ask the Holy Spirit to reveal to you any identity lies you believe about yourself based on the incident.
6. Renounce the identity lie: "In the name of Jesus Christ, I renounce the lie that I am not loved or cared for, that I have to perform well to be loved, and so forth."
7. Announce the truth of your identity in Christ: "In the name of Jesus Christ, I announce the truth that I am seen, that I am valuable, that I am loved, and so forth."
8. Bring the person with you to meet Jesus on the Cross at Calvary; look at his face of care and mercy.
9. Ask Jesus to forgive the person.
10. Ask Jesus to give you the grace to forgive the person.
11. Pray a prayer of blessing for that person. Ask God to bless them and heal them on their journey.
12. Ask Jesus to seal this forgiveness and heal the wounds in your life.
13. Thank God for his healing mercy and grace.

FIFTH WEEK OF LENT

SATURDAY

CHRIST WAS HANDED OVER,
BUT TO GATHER INTO ONE THE
CHILDREN OF GOD WHO ARE
SCATTERED ABROAD.

JOHN 11:51–52

THE SACRAMENT OF RECONCILIATION

"It is there, in fact, 'in the depths of the heart,' that everything is bound and loosed. It is not in our power not to feel or to forget an offense. But the heart that offers itself to the Holy Spirit turns injury into compassion and purifies the memory in transforming the hurt into intercession" (*CCC* 2843). A marvelous exchange takes place in the process of forgiveness. We offer to Jesus our pain, agony, bitterness, and hardened hearts, and he takes our offering, brings it to his heart upon the Cross on which he hangs, and in return offers us mercy for the forgiveness of our own sins, healing from the sins others have committed against us, and the restoration of our lives.

He takes our lives, unites them with his, and gives us his very self. In every moment of suffering he is with us. He is the way through. And only in the daily living of the Paschal Mystery with Christ do we find true life.

In the divine economy of salvation, nothing is wasted. Everything we surrender to Jesus is transformed unto glory. It all matters. All of it.

As a conclusion to our Lenten journey and our meditations on prayer, fasting, and almsgiving, and as we enter into Holy Week, I want to sincerely and seriously invite you to go to the Sacrament of Reconciliation this week. Please.

There is nothing else on earth that equals a good sacramental confession where our sins are forgiven; where our hearts, minds, bodies, and souls are healed; and where the enemy of our salvation, Satan the sniper, is vanquished. In the sacrament of Confession, through the words of absolution from the priest, Christ's heart of forgiveness and mercy is made known and we can stand firm in the certitude of the forgiveness of our sins. This closes the door to the enemy and simultaneously brings us into communion with God, ourselves, and others. There is nothing else like it.

No matter how long it has been since your last Confession, please go. The priest will help you if you don't know what to do. Bring everything that you have encountered these weeks and go. Go and be free. Go and find peace.

REFLECT

What sins keep you from freedom and peace?

_____

_____

_____

_____

_____

_____

_____

_____

_____

_____

_____

_____

_____

_____

_____

_____

_____

_____

_____

_____

_____

_____

_____

PRAY

*LORD, THANK YOU FOR LOVING ME.
THANK YOU FOR BEING THE WAY, THE
TRUTH, AND THE LIFE. AMEN.*

PART 4

SACRIFICE

JESUS TAKES ON OUR SIN AND DEATH AND RESTORES US TO LIFE

HE WILL PROVIDE THE WAY AND THE MEANS, SUCH AS YOU COULD NEVER HAVE IMAGINED. LEAVE IT ALL TO HIM, LET GO OF YOURSELF, LOSE YOURSELF ON THE CROSS, AND YOU WILL FIND YOURSELF ENTIRELY.

ST. CATHERINE OF SIENA

HOLY WEEK, THE WEEK OF ALL WEEKS

HOLY WEEK

PALM SUNDAY

HOSANNA TO THE SON OF DAVID! BLESSED IS HE WHO COMES IN THE NAME OF THE LORD!

MATTHEW 21:9

OUR LORD'S PASSION

This is a week unlike any other week. This is the week that Jesus makes the offering of himself, reconciling everything to the Father. This is the week that love is poured out in fullness. This week changes everything. This week the power of sin, hell, and death is destroyed. This is the week that the pathway is opened to eternal life. This week is for every single one us, for the heart of Christ is for every single one of us.

St. Gregory of Nyssa proclaims, "Sick, our nature demanded to be healed; fallen, to be raised up; dead, to rise again. We had lost the possession of the good; it was necessary for it to be given back to us. Closed in the darkness, it was necessary to bring us the light; captives, we awaited a Savior; prisoners, help; slaves, a liberator. Are these things minor or insignificant? Did they not move God to descend to human nature and visit it, since humanity was in so miserable and unhappy a state?" (*CCC* 457).

Jesus is hailed on Sunday and crucified on Friday. How fickle the heart of humankind. And yet Christ willingly and with endless love makes the journey for us all. He will give his life for those who will respond and receive eternal life, embracing his own life and heart and entering into his Father's kingdom, which is heaven. And Jesus will give his life for those who will not receive him, who will turn away, and who will choose the way of eternal separation, which is hell.

Jesus said yes to the will of the Father, the way of salvation and life.

Will we? The choice is ours.

REFLECT

Imagine yourself on the side of the road watching Jesus begin his journey toward Jerusalem. You see people spreading their cloaks and palm branches on the ground as he approaches, and you hear their shouts of gladness. As you watch him, perhaps with a palm branch in your own hand as well, what do you notice happening in your heart?

_____

_____

_____

_____

_____

_____

_____

_____

_____

_____

_____

_____

_____

_____

_____

_____

_____

_____

_____

_____

_____

_____

_____

PRAY

JESUS, TAKE ME WITH YOU THIS
WEEK. TAKE ME WITH YOU IN
EVERY MOMENT OF YOUR LIFE IN
THESE DAYS. KEEP ME FOCUSED
AND FAITHFUL TO WHAT TRULY
MATTERS—YOU.

HOLY WEEK

MONDAY

GRANT, WE PRAY, ALMIGHTY
GOD,
THAT, THOUGH IN OUR
WEAKNESS WE FAIL,
WE MAY BE REVIVED THROUGH
THE PASSION OF YOUR ONLY
BEGOTTEN SON.

COLLECT FOR MASS OF THE DAY

REVEAL YOUR HEART

"Actions speak louder than words" is an adage we are familiar with. We know someone loves us or cares for us not just by hearing them say it (which is important) but also by actions that reinforce and augment the words that are spoken. As our emotions reveal what we believe in our heart about a situation, our actions reveal our heart in magnanimity or miserliness. Our behavior flows from what we truly believe.

We see the manifestation of heart today in Judas and Mary of Bethany from the Gospel of John 12:1–11. Mary takes a liter (a tremendous amount) of costly perfumed oil made from genuine aromatic nard and anoints the feet of Jesus and dries them with her hair (a deeply humble and intimate act of love). Her offering is so rich, generous, and extravagant that the entire house is filled with the fragrance of the oil. Some surmise that the offering of that expensive oil was part of her own family inheritance that she lavishes on Jesus. Nothing is wasted on Jesus.

Judas is present in the house as well, and when Judas sees the rich offering and extravagant gift literally poured out upon Jesus, his stingy and duplicitous words reveal the darkness of his heart that is manifested in the theft of the offerings of others.

The world does not understand a heart poured out for Jesus. The world considers it a waste, an outrage, ludicrous. How many people, young and old, have revealed their love for Christ, only to be met with scorn and ridicule, many times by their own families? Christ understands this. His answer to Judas is not one of correction for Mary but a defense of her. "Leave her alone," he says. Her love is preparing him for his death.

REFLECT

Where within your heart do you see the tendency of the generous heart of Mary? Where is your love for Christ poured out? What are the actions in your life that reveal your heart?

PRAY

*LORD, GIVE ME A GENEROUS AND
OPEN HEART. MAY MY LOVE FOR
YOU GROW MORE DEEPLY INTO A
FRAGRANT, LIFE-GIVING AROMA THAT
FILLS THE WORLD AROUND ME.*

HOLY WEEK

TUESDAY

PETER SAID TO HIM, "LORD, WHY
CAN I NOT FOLLOW YOU NOW?
I WILL LAY DOWN MY LIFE FOR
YOU."

JOHN 13:37

STAND FIRM IN TRUTH

I love St. Peter. I love his passion, his brashness, his simple understanding. And more than that, I love his unveiled heart. Peter will catastrophically fail Jesus on Thursday night, but he doesn't know it yet. He sees Jesus and himself in a paradigm that is about to be shattered. We all know what this is like. We have all surprised ourselves by the incongruity of our words, sentiments, and actions. We have all done things we swore we would never do, and we have all broken promises we said we would keep. Given our frail humanity, the question is not so much if we will sin or fail, but where we will turn our face when we do. To whom shall we go?

When Peter is confronted with his threefold denial and failure and is cloaked in the shame of his own betrayal, Jesus turns toward him and looks directly at him. Peter meets his gaze and his heart bursts forth in tears of anguish and sorrow (see Luke 22:60–62). His bitter tears begin a ripe repentance. Jesus is so good to Peter and so attentive to his heart and the damage he did to himself by his own denial that Jesus will set up another scene by a charcoal fire, this one leading to a threefold affirmation of love and restoration (see John 21:9–19). Nothing is wasted on Jesus. Jesus uses everything in our lives to bring about restoration if we allow him to do so.

Where within your heart do you see the tendency of the weakness of Peter? Where is it easiest in your life for you to deny Jesus? Be very honest. Where is Jesus meeting you there in love and truth, gazing upon you and calling you to repentance?

PRAY

JESUS, PLEASE FORGIVE ME FOR ALL
THE WAYS I DENY YOU AND SHRINK
BACK IN FEAR FROM HARD TRUTHS.
PLEASE ROOT ME AND GROUND ME
IN YOUR LOVE SO THAT I CAN STAND
FIRM IN YOU, COME WHAT MAY.

HOLY WEEK

WEDNESDAY

MORNING BY MORNING HE
WAKENS, HE WAKENS MY EAR
TO HEAR AS THOSE WHO
ARE TAUGHT. THE LORD HAS
OPENED MY EAR, AND I WAS NOT
REBELLIOUS, I TURNED NOT
BACKWARD.

ISAIAH 50:4–5

DISPEL ALL DARKNESS

Jesus Christ is the fullness of man. He is the new Adam. He is the way, the truth, and the life. He is the beloved Son, the divine bridegroom, the Good Shepherd. Jesus is Savior, Lord, Friend, the Christ. He is the Messiah, Lamb of God, King of kings.

Jesus is the Word (Logos), the light of the world, Emmanuel, God with us. "In the beginning was the Word, and the Word was with God, and the Word was God. He was in the beginning with God; all things were made through him, and without him was not anything made that was made. In him was life, and the life was the light of men. The light shines in the darkness, and the darkness has not overcome it" (Jn 1:1–5).

This light, Christ himself, is the one who loves us, who purifies us, and who protects and heals us. This is the one who, in the next few days to come, will give his life for us.

He is true God and true man.

The darkness did not overcome him; and in him, it will not overcome us.

REFLECT

What arises in your heart as you read and pray through John
1:1–5?

_____

_____

_____

_____

_____

_____

_____

_____

_____

_____

_____

_____

_____

_____

_____

_____

_____

_____

_____

_____

_____

_____

_____

_____

PRAY

COME, LORD JESUS, WITH YOUR
LIGHT TO DISPEL THE DARKNESS OF
MY HEART.

191

HOLY WEEK

HOLY THURSDAY

[JESUS CHRIST HAS] MADE US
INTO A KINGDOM, PRIESTS TO
HIS GOD AND FATHER, TO HIM
BE GLORY AND DOMINION FOR
EVER AND EVER. AMEN.

REVELATION 1:6

PRIESTLY POWER

This is the night that Jesus will be given over for our sins and begin his Passion. The Mass that we celebrate on the evening of the Lord's Supper is the last Mass that will be prayed before Easter Vigil. In this Mass, Jesus will offer bread and wine as his Body and Blood, and he will tell the disciples, "Do this in memory of me." Jesus institutes the ministerial priesthood at this moment, and for more than two thousand years, priests have been offering bread and wine that become the Body and Blood of Christ, saying the exact words of Jesus in the power of the Holy Spirit.

This priesthood, shared from the one priesthood of Jesus Christ, is an unfathomable gift from God. God chooses certain men to share in his life to offer sacrifice for all. He invites them into his heart to be configured to him, indelibly marking their soul and ontologically changing them to act in the person of Christ (*in persona Christi*).

Jesus gives these chosen men the ability to confect the Eucharist, absolve sins in the sacrament of Confession, anoint the sick, and shepherd his people. Because of their configuration to Christ, priests literally love in a way that no one else can love. They love with the heart of Christ the bridegroom poured out for his bride, the Church. They love with the heart of the Good Shepherd, who guides and leads the flock. They love with the heart of the Divine Physician as they heal the sickness of sin and prepare people for death.

The very being of a priest emanates the magnificence and steadfast care and protection of Christ and the fidelity of God who never leaves us or forsakes us. The glory and beauty of the priesthood is beyond words. If men stopped saying yes to the invitation of Jesus Christ to become his priests, the world would cease to exist as we know it.

We must pray for our priests. We must fast for them. We must encourage them and speak the truth to them in love. We must pray that many men have the courage to search their hearts to discover if Jesus has given them this gift of an extraordinary life completely poured out in loving service of the bride, the Church. There is nothing else like it.

REFLECT

Men, please search your hearts and ask God if he is calling you to this life. You will never regret saying yes to Jesus. It will be the best thing you ever do. We need you.

Women, please search your hearts and ask God how you can support vocations to the priesthood, as well as priests currently in ministry. You might dedicate time in your personal and family prayer for these men, or you could reach out with a note of affirmation to the good priests who have helped you grow in your spiritual life.

_____

_____

_____

_____

_____

_____

_____

_____

_____

PRAY

JESUS, PLEASE BLESS YOUR PRIESTS.
YOU LOVE THEM, AND YOU HAVE
CHOSEN THEM. PLEASE HEAL THEM
AND ENCOURAGE THEM, AND GIVE
THEM THE ZEAL AND LOVE OF YOUR
HEART. MAY THEY KNOW THAT THEIR
HOME IS IN YOU AND THAT THEY
BELONG TO YOU FOREVER. AMEN.

IT IS FINISHED.

JOHN 19:30

SURRENDER

Good Friday. The great equalizer of humankind. Rich, poor, young, old, powerful, weak—all kneel before the Cross of Jesus Christ. There are no words. In the noisy chaos of Jerusalem, crowds, political struggles, and the lament of Calvary, a silence reigns midafternoon on that great and terrible day.

What can be said as we gaze upon him? What can be said as we behold the Man, broken and bloodied?

> He was despised and rejected by men;
>> a man of sorrows, and acquainted with grief;
> and as one from whom men hide their faces
>> he was despised, and we esteemed him not.
> Surely he has borne our griefs
>> and carried our sorrows;
> yet we esteemed him stricken,
>> struck down by God, and afflicted.
> But he was wounded for our transgressions,
>> he was bruised for our iniquities;
> upon him was the chastisement that made us whole,
>> and by his stripes we are healed. (Is 53:3–5)

REFLECT

What griefs and sorrows do you surrender to Christ? Which sins do you lay at the foot of the Cross?

_____

_____

_____

_____

_____

_____

_____

_____

_____

_____

_____

PRAY

*FATHER, FORGIVE THEM, FOR THEY
KNOW NOT WHAT THEY DO. JESUS,
HEAL ME. I SURRENDER TO YOU.*

HOLY SATURDAY

AND JOSEPH TOOK THE BODY,
AND WRAPPED IT IN A CLEAN
LINEN SHROUD, AND LAID IT IN
HIS OWN NEW TOMB, WHICH HE
HAD HEWN IN THE ROCK; AND
HE ROLLED A GREAT STONE TO
THE DOOR OF THE TOMB, AND
DEPARTED. MARY MAG'DALENE
AND THE OTHER MARY WERE
THERE, SITTING OPPOSITE THE
TOMB.

MATTHEW 27:59–61

BE STILL

Today is a day of great stillness. We keenly feel the death of Christ, who now sleeps in a tomb. The earth is quiet. In this quiet as we experience the ache for Jesus, we sometimes don't quite know what to do with ourselves.

An ancient homily on Holy Saturday captures it best: "What is happening? Today there is a great silence over the earth, a great silence, and stillness, a great silence because the King sleeps; the earth was in terror and was still, because God slept in the flesh and raised up those who were sleeping from the ages. God has died in the flesh, and the underworld has trembled."

Heaven and earth wait in silence as Christ makes his journey.

The homily continues: "Truly he goes to seek out our first parent like a lost sheep; he wishes to visit those who sit in darkness and in the shadow of death. He goes to free the prisoner Adam and his fellow prisoner Eve from their pains, he who is God, and Adam's son. The Lord goes in to them holding his victorious weapon, his Cross. When Adam, the first created man, sees him, he strikes his breast in terror and calls out to all: 'My Lord be with you all.' And Christ in reply says to Adam: 'And with your spirit.' And grasping his hand he raises him up, saying, 'Awake, O sleeper, and arise from the dead, and Christ shall give you light.'"

This is the path of all of us, dear friends. This is the path from death to life. This is what Lent has been all about—becoming one with the One who will grasp us by the hand and say to us, "Awake and arise!"

This life is not the end. This life is not all there is. The best things on earth are only a small foreshadowing of the beauty of heaven.

What experiences in this life have given you glimpses of the joy of eternal life? How can you live that joy more fully each day?

_____

_____

_____

_____

_____

_____

_____

_____

_____

_____

_____

PRAY

_FATHER, HELP ME TO SEE THE TRUTH
ABOUT THIS LIFE AND THE NEXT.
AMEN._

EASTER SUNDAY

THIS IS THE NIGHT,
WHEN CHRIST BROKE THE
    PRISON-BARS OF DEATH
AND ROSE VICTORIOUS FROM
    THE UNDERWORLD. . . .
O TRULY NECESSARY SIN OF
    ADAM,
DESTROYED COMPLETELY BY
    THE DEATH OF CHRIST!
O HAPPY FAULT
THAT EARNED SO GREAT, SO
    GLORIOUS A REDEEMER!

EXSULTET FROM THE EASTER VIGIL

THE FULLNESS
OF ALL THINGS

The Easter Vigil Mass is the greatest and highest of all solemnities. It takes place after the sun sets on Saturday and is truly glorious in every way. It begins with the blessing of a new fire outside the church and the preparation of the paschal candle. I would like to offer the words the priest says during the preparation of the paschal candle as a summary of the journey we have made this Lent.

As he cuts a cross and the Greek letters alpha and omega into the candle, he says,

> Christ yesterday and today
> the Beginning and the End
> the Alpha
> and the Omega
> All time belongs to him
> and all the ages
> To him be glory and power
> through every age and forever. Amen.

The priest then inserts five grains of incense into the candle in the form of a cross and says,

> By his holy
> and glorious wounds,
> may Christ the Lord
> guard us
> and protect us. Amen.

And then the priest lights the paschal candle from the new fire, saying,

> May the light of Christ rising in glory
> dispel the darkness of our hearts and minds.

This is the fullness of all things.

God is sovereign. All time, every moment of our lives, belongs to him. Nothing is outside the grasp of God. It is by his glorious wounds that he heals us, guards us, and protects us. And it is the light of Christ that dispels the darkness of our hearts and minds. And may it always be so.

We are not slaves to sin and death. We are children of God. We belong to him. These days of prayer, fasting, and almsgiving are a means of communion with God, ourselves, and others. This is the way home. The only way is through Jesus Christ—the Way, the Truth, and the Life. Forever.

Jesus Christ is risen. Truly, he is risen. And so are you.

For the days ahead:

As we go forth . . .

Thank you for coming along on this journey. I pray it has blessed you and opened new doors into your heart and life.

As we begin the Easter season, I would like to invite you to take time and particularly note the graces Jesus gave you during Lent, and I would like to invite you to ask him how he wants you to continue on this path.

Because love never ends, we are always learning and growing, forgiving and being forgiven. The narrow way is not easy, but we are not alone, and with Jesus we can do all things through him who strengthens us (see Philippians 4:13).

You are so loved, dear friends. So deeply loved. As I wrote the words of this book, countless times many faces came to my mind and heart, and I prayed for every single one of you who would read it and make the journey.

Hopefully we will all meet one another in eternity, in the love and joy and beauty that never ends.

BLESSINGS AND PEACE,
SR. MIRIAM JAMES HEIDLAND

SR. MIRIAM JAMES HEIDLAND, SOLT, is a popular Catholic speaker, cohost of the *Abiding Together* podcast, and the author of the bestselling book *Loved as I Am*.

A former Division I athlete who had a radical conversion and joined the Society of Our Lady of the Most Holy Trinity in 1998, Heidland has shared her story on EWTN's *The Journey Home*, at numerous SEEK and Steubenville conferences, and at the USC-CB's Convocation of Catholic Leaders.

In addition to speaking, Heidland has served in parish ministry and as the director of novices for her SOLT community. She also has served as an assistant to both her provincial and general superiors.

Heidland earned a master's degree in theology from the Augustine Institute and speaks extensively on the topics of conversion, authentic love, forgiveness, and healing.

VALERIE DELGADO is a Catholic painter, a digital artist, and the owner of Pax.Beloved. She illustrated the book *Adore* by Fr. John Burns and *ABC Get to Know the Saints with Me* by Caroline Perkins.

She lives in the Houston, Texas, area.

www.paxbeloved.com
Instagram: @pax.valerie